21 DAYS

of

TRANSFORMING
PRAYER

How Everything Changes When
You Seek God's Face

21 DAYS

of

TRANSFORMING PRAYER

How Everything Changes When
You Seek God's Face

DANIEL HENDERSON

WITH JIM MAXIM AND ALICE MOSS

STRATEGIC RENEWAL

© 2021 by Daniel Henderson

Published by Strategic Renewal

www.strategicrenewal.com

Printed in the United States of America

ISBN 9780981609065

Emphasis in Scripture shown by italics is the author's.

Contents

Foreword

At this critical point in Church history, there is little time for Christians to be distracted over secondary issues. The challenges of a growing secularization that disparages the Gospel of Christ are all too evident to every believer. The Christian Church must be stirred to arise and live out the calling Jesus gave us as salt and light.

But how can we see a radical change in the spiritual landscape without a radical return to prayer and the Word by the Body of Christ? Human resources and church growth novelties that lead us away from these essentials always prove ineffective at best—and spiritually destructive at worst. Only something sent from Heaven itself will overcome the darkness around us so Christ can be seen as the world's only hope.

Every believer knows that the Bible is clear about prayer. God's House will be called a house of prayer. Preaching is essential. Praise, worship, and fellowship are important component parts of the work of the Lord, but His House will be called a house of prayer. Why? Because when believers come to the throne of grace and start seeking God with all their hearts, God has promised—and He can never fail this promise. He has said, "When you call, I will answer. Ask and you will receive, seek and you will find, knock and the door will be opened to you." When this happens, we are going to see God come and give a renewal of the spirit of prayer, the burden of prayer, and strategies so that all our churches can be houses of prayer.

Daniel Henderson has been commissioned by God to inspire pastors and churches across the nation to reconsider and commit to Acts 6:4: "But we will devote ourselves to prayer and to the ministry of the word" (ESV). God is wonderfully using Daniel to bring believers together around the country, across denominational lines, to pray for one another and to encourage prayer in our individual churches. This is one of those vital things happening in the Body of Christ that is going to bring more of God's blessing in our lives and that will mean the name of Christ will be glorified more than ever before.

As you read *21 Days of Transforming Prayer*, open your heart to God's voice. You will be both encouraged and inspired to believe again that with God, nothing is impossible.

Jim Cymbala
The Brooklyn Tabernacle

Introduction

The Road to Real Change

Praying Christians never forget the first time they sought the face of God and experienced the power of a transforming spiritual intimacy. For me, it occurred during my college years. It was a Friday night. I was alone in my dorm room, which was highly unusual as I was typically busy with school activities and dating.

Looking back, I realize the Holy Spirit had been preparing my heart for this moment, as is the case for most believers. The account of Moses speaking to God in deep intimacy "face to face, as a man speaks to his friend" (Exodus 33:11) had recently captivated my heart. One of my professors had been speaking of those times in his life when the Presence of God felt so real that if he had opened his eyes, it seemed he would be staring God in the face. Honestly, I had never experienced that kind of moment.

That night, as I sat in my simple dorm room, these realities converged as the Holy Spirit stirred my heart with a strange and new spiritual hunger. I found myself flat on my face, pouring out my passionate gratitude and worship to the Savior who knew me, walked with me, guided me, taught me, and loved me with a tender and attentive heart. In those moments, the presence, provision, and power of God in my life became real. Truly, I felt that if I had opened my eyes, I would have been looking at the Holy One ... face to face.

My Confessional

Even though I am sharing this 21-Day resource on prayer, I need to confess up front that I am not a natural "prayer guy." You see, prayer is essentially depending on God—and I have a fiercely independent personality. I say often that prayerlessness is our declaration of independence from God. I get that. It is very easy for me to forge ahead on Christian autopilot, relying on the reserves of previous learning and last week's worship and not abiding in Christ in a constant, moment-by-moment reliance. Beyond this, it is easy to ignore the opportunities for community prayer, thinking I do not need it, or viewing it as a gathering of folks who have nothing else more productive to do with their time.

Longing for More

Many people share my struggle. In fact, through thirty-plus years of pastoral ministry, I've discovered that most Christians are secretly discouraged with prayer. We look around the church and assume everyone else must be praying more and better than we are. With rare exception, they are not.

Deep within, we know there is another dimension of Christian living beyond a cultural faith that simply checks in with God at church or in times of crisis. We are tired of feeling bored, inept, confused, frustrated, or weary, in any sense, with the idea of prayer. We envision the power of the living Christ and His Gospel inflaming our hearts to serve as agents of real transformation in this society. We yearn for real change but know that somehow, it must begin within us.

My Goal for this Journey

I am passionate about helping you discover what I have seen thousands experience as they have learned the power of an approach to prayer that is truly transformational. As I write, I can imagine a Spirit-instigated tidal wave of engaging and enduring prayer that changes our lives as "times of refreshing" come from the Presence of the Lord. I hope you will imagine with me as we journey together into a renewed understanding of the power of Christ, who can still transform our lives and our world through the reality of prayer.

Daniel Henderson

Beyond a "Grocery List" of Needs

We all learn many of the essential skills of life through the model of others we love and respect. Some skills allow us to excel and become contributors to others. However, we can also learn ineptitude through the repetition of mindless tradition or dysfunction.

This leads to a core inquiry. Who taught you to pray? Has anyone provided a positive and life-changing model of prayer for you? Do you feel that you even know how to pray effectively? What is the purpose behind your praying? Is it working for you? Are you sure it is a Biblical approach? Are you simply doing what you have seen others do, wondering if there might be more to the reality of prayer than you have experienced so far in your life?

The "request-based" approach to prayer that was modeled to me during traditional "prayer meetings" just did not work for me. This dissatisfaction led me to a growing, life-changing understanding of what I call "worship-based prayer." It was not a new discovery but a simple revelation of what is clear in the Scriptures as a positive alternative to "grocery-list" praying. This approach has transformed my life and the lives of thousands I have encountered who have made this vital discovery.

What is Worship-Based Prayer?

Worship is the response of all we are to the revelation of all God is. J. Oswald Sanders describes worship as "the loving ascription of praise to God for what He is, both in Himself and in His ways. It is the bowing of innermost spirit in deep humility and reverence before Him." [1]

"Worship-based prayer" seeks the face of God before the hand of God. God's face is the essence of who He is. God's hand is the blessing of what He does. God's face represents His person and presence. God's hand expresses His provision for needs in our lives. I have learned that if all we ever do is seek God's hand, we may miss His face; but if we seek His face, He will be glad to open His hand and satisfy the deepest desires of our hearts.

This approach to prayer always begins with a focus on Biblical, Spirit-empowered worship. It is distinctively different than the traditional approach that emphasizes prayer requests and long lists of needs as the foundation of prayer. Christ taught a worship-based approach to prayer. It is modeled by many Biblical personalities. It is fueled by Scriptural truth in every case. Worship-based prayer ignites a desire for spiritual intimacy and personal transformation. In this discovery, a Christian is then empowered and enlightened to pray about issues and needs in a whole new way.

What Worship-Based Prayer is Not

As you prepare for this journey in the principles and practices of worship-based prayer, let me tell you what worship-based prayer is NOT.

• It is not a new method of prayer. While the discovery has been fresh for many in this generation, it is an approach to prayer that is as old as the Scriptures.

• It is not worship-ONLY prayer. Biblical, balanced prayer has many expressions. This is not about restricting your prayer life only to worship but about rekindling your prayer life from a foundation of worship to more fully enjoy and experience confession, requests, intercession, and warfare prayers.

• It does not eliminate requests. Our Father commands and compels us to call on Him—and He promises to answer. Requests are a vital part of prayer. However, requests without the proper foundation and framework can miss the mark. Worship-based prayer helps us understand the context, conditions, and ultimate conclusion of all our prayer requests.

• It is not complicated. While the term may sound a bit different, the approach is not difficult. Ultimately, it is as pure as opening the Scriptures and the soul in Spirit-led communion with Christ and allowing Him to set the agenda for every prayer time you enjoy.

A Transformation Story

As a pastor, I have seen first-hand the power of worship-based prayer to bring healing and restoration to hurting congregations. I have watched it reinvent a staid, traditional church into a church-planting, mission-oriented force. Most thrilling is the fact that thousands of believers have experienced a revived love for Christ and a renewed passion for Spirit-empowered ministry.

In October 1995, Lori gave her life to Jesus Christ. A few months later, she signed up to attend a prayer event sponsored by the women of our church. They were going away to pray for three days, with no agenda. This was a big stretch for a baby Christian.

At the time, her song repertoire consisted of the chorus of "Amazing Grace" and "Jesus Loves Me." She writes, "I wouldn't have been able to find a book of the Bible other than Genesis if you'd paid me. And as you might imagine, I would never dream of lifting up my hands as I had seen once in one of those 'weird churches.' "

However, God used that weekend to transform her life. She learned how to open the Bible and worship God as the majestic, sovereign, and mighty One who is worthy of praise. She saw Him take hurting people and give them peace, hope, and joy. Her life has never been the same.

In the ensuing years, Lori became the ministry director of Strategic Renewal, the non-profit organization I founded, teaching the principles of worship-based prayer to hundreds of churches around the nation. Today, she leads the prayer ministry at a growing congregation in Northern California. God is using her in profound ways. Blessings continue to pour into her life, family, and ministry all because one day, as a new believer, she stepped into a praying church and encountered a life-transforming moment in His Presence.

Join us in prayer for Day 1
at www.strategicrenewal.com/21days

DAY 2

The Potential for Transformation

Too many times, we become preoccupied with the tools, techniques, and even the finer points of theology when it comes to prayer. All of these are helpful, but prayer is not so much an issue of fine-tuning the regimens but of enjoying the relationship. It is not so much about fixing all the peripheral issues of our lives through prayer but allowing God to change us through prayer. When we get things right on the inside, by His transforming grace, it is amazing how so many other things seem to line up and make sense.

The Fruit of Transforming Prayer

As I have watched the power of worship-based prayer transform hundreds of lives, I have seen some very specific fruit. I long for more of this fruit in my life and the lives of everyone I influence. I grieve when I fall short of this fruit. I pray for a greater vision and passion for this fruit in my life and the lives of others.

What does this fruit look like? Here is a summary of what I have seen occur as people learn to seek God's face:

God is glorified!—One of the great results of transforming prayer is that people recognize God at work because they have joined Him in that work through their prayers. Their hearts are sensitized to His Presence, His power, and His purposes. Their lips are free to recognize Him as the source of all good things. Their hearts are eager to cry out, "Not unto us, O LORD, not unto us, but to Your name give glory!" (Psalms 115:1).

For people who fail to pray, everything is a coincidence that has little recognition of God at work. For those who pray, everything is a co-incident, as they have joined the Lord in His work through the privilege of prayer.

I am sanctified!—*Sanctified.* Did you notice that word in the morning paper today? Of course not. It is not a word in common use, but it packs a powerful meaning. It means to be "set apart" to God. It means God is working in me, around me, and through me to make me holy, more like Jesus.

The great fruit of transforming prayer is that praying Christians, while not perfect, are growing every day to the point that they act, think, speak, and serve like Jesus.

The church is edified!—When I first came to the church Northern in California, I followed a godly predecessor who served for forty years as their senior pastor. This left a great heritage, for which I was very grateful. It also left a very traditional, older church. These wonderful saints cherished the days of the past and felt trepidation as they faced the inevitability of change in the future.

Five years later, at one of our conferences, a visiting pastor from New York commented, "These are the youngest old people I have ever seen." This was evidence that when transformation occurs within hearts, ignited by the truth and Presence of Christ, everything else begins to change for the sake of the health of the church and the fulfillment of the mission. To say that the church is "edified" means that the lives, marriages, families, and ministries of the church are built up, made strong and healthy—through Biblical prayer, in the power of the Holy Spirit.

The world is mystified!—Over the years, we have heard significant debate about the best way to reach the unchurched and what influences the hearts of unbelievers who attend our church services. First Corinthians 14:25 is the only verse in the New Testament that speaks specifically to the experience of an unbeliever coming into a church service. In essence, when the Spirit is working among God's people, and the truth is honored in their midst, it says that the unbeliever sees this in the lives of believers and "the secrets of his heart are revealed; and so, falling down on his face, he will worship God and report that God is truly among you." I believe this a clear description of the glory (manifest presence) of Christ among His people.

Ultimately, the world is always transformed by sanctified Christians through whom the life of Jesus becomes a mystifying manifestation. As Paul said, "For it is the God who commanded light to shine out of darkness, who has shone in our hearts to give the light of the knowledge of the glory of God in the face of Jesus Christ. But we have this treasure in earthen vessels, that the excellence of the power may be of God and not of us" (2 Corinthians 4:6–7). People changed by Jesus cannot help but change the world.

The enemy is notified!—This is not a book on spiritual warfare, but I want to remind you that Satan is not omniscient. He is supernatural and powerful and supported by myriads of demonic forces, but he cannot read our thoughts. The best he can do is observe our behavior, eavesdrop on our conversations, and implement a strategy to send his fiery darts against our minds—based on his understanding of our vulnerabilities and habits.

When we are in the habit of experiencing transformation as we seek God's face, the enemy's efforts to defeat, discourage, distract, or destroy us are met with the reality of our Christ-ward focus and the victory that comes from intimacy with Jesus. To Satan's dismay, he sees us praying, trusting God, and becoming more like our Lord as we do so. Satan is notified that we are engaged in pursuit of the promises of transformation and impact for the Savior.

Join us in prayer for Day 2
at www.strategicrenewal.com/21days

What Is Blocking the Breakthrough?

Let's be honest. Most of us struggle to feel satisfied in our prayer lives. The great promises of prayer are true, but many don't experience them. Even pastors are trying to find their way when it comes to prayer. One study found that only 16 percent of Protestant ministers across the country are very satisfied with their personal prayer life. Another 47 percent are somewhat satisfied; 30 percent are somewhat dissatisfied; and 7 percent are very dissatisfied with their prayer lives.[1]

Barriers to Blessing

If prayer is such a vital tool for transformation, why is it so difficult for so many people? Why does this divinely intended blessing remain a burden for many believers?

Spiritual Warfare

Clearly, prayer is an area where believers experience spiritual warfare. Our spiritual enemy is fully aware of the power and promises available to us in prayer. He knows that every major spiritual revival began with prayer. He knows we are all called to be "praying menaces" to his cause. Therefore, he fights us from every angle to keep us from praying effectively.

Fear of Intimacy

Some falter in prayer because of a fear of intimacy. Some of us still carry the baggage from parents or other authority figures in our childhood who were distant, negligent, or even abusive. These experiences can leave us with distaste for emotional vulnerability and transparency. We protect ourselves from getting too close to anyone, even God. Others simply embrace erroneous views of God's character that keep them at a distance from their self-styled deity who is mysteriously remote, unpredictably angry, and impossible to please.

Misguided Focus

Many of us maintain a misguided focus in our prayers and miss the life-giving reality God intended. Instead of our first resolve, we view prayer as our last resort. We see prayer as our spiritual e-mail sent to God, with instructions as to how He should manage the affairs of our lives each day. We attempt to use prayer to get our will done in Heaven rather than His will done on earth. But at any point in our lives, the Lord can refocus our prayers with powerful results.

Counterproductive Tradition

Countless believers have learned to pray, from a counterproductive tradition, forms of prayer passed down through the generations without much critical evaluation and Biblical investigation. Some traditions in prayer rely mainly on "prayer lists" and others on rote expressions, rather than upon the leading of the Holy Spirit.

Boredom

All of these factors can fuel a deep-seated feeling of boredom. As a Christ-follower for over fifty years, I am resolute to banish boredom from my prayer life. Yet many of us have all but given up our high expectations of prayer. For many, prayer has become a real yawner—and that has to change before transformation can occur.

Lack of Positive Models

One colossal reason we have not experienced transforming prayer is the lack of positive models. I have learned that people do not arrive at a new, powerful, and life-changing place in their prayer life through information. It happens more by "infection." It is not accomplished through explanation but by experience.

Contexts for Breakthrough

For the past decade, I have taken hundreds of fellow leaders, church members, and students to the Tuesday night prayer meetings at The Brooklyn Tabernacle. It is not the only model but probably the most compelling example of a church in the United States where believers really know how to pray. (Alternatively, there are countless models in other countries like South Korea and in areas of the world where Christians face persecution, like China.) Under the leadership of Pastor Jim Cymbala, four thousand gather every Tuesday night, simply to seek the Lord and enjoy the abundance of His Presence. Prayer is the engine that drives all the ministries of this high-impact church.

I heard a Brazilian proverb years ago: "The heart cannot taste what the eyes have not seen." This experience of praying with a pastor, church, and congregation that authentically value the priority and power of prayer has accomplished much to help me and many other believers understand a truly Biblical paradigm.

Today, my passion is to serve as a "spiritual pyromaniac," traveling to churches and conferences, demonstrating the power of seeking God's face and leading prayer experiences that establish a fresh, life-transforming approach to prayer. This is my small way of serving others with some modeling and mentoring experiences. It is exhilarating beyond words, week after week, to see the lights come on for people who discover that the promises and power of prayer can be real—and that prayer can change things, starting with our own hearts.

Perhaps you are longing for lasting alterations in your spiritual journey and life direction as you learn to seek the face of God. The promises are real. The potential is unfathomable. The principles are proven. Christ is extending the invitation to your heart. Right here. Right now.

Join us in prayer for Day 3
at www.strategicrenewal.com/21days

Face Time!

I love "face time"— with certain people. When I get face time with my wife, children, family members, and good friends, it is always meaningful and enriching. Of course, I also dread face time with certain people.

Face time can be good or bad, depending on who we are facing and the nature of the encounter. The idea of God's face is one of the most powerful, life-changing themes in the Bible. Still, many live their entire lives with minimal emphasis on face time with God. Perhaps they don't understand the incredible opportunity because they've never experienced it. Maybe they don't feel the need. Maybe prayer time is just too rushed. But face time with God is the refreshment the human soul so desperately needs. And like temperature, pulse, and blood pressure tests we encounter when we visit the doctor, face time tells us how we are really doing. If we get nothing else from this book, we must get this.

What's in a Face?

What is meant by *face*? It is the representation of the real essence and character of a person. It is the unique identifying characteristic of an individual. It is also the key to really getting to know someone. Proverbs 15:13 says, "A happy heart makes the face cheerful" (NIV). Just as the eyes are the windows to the soul, so a face is the canvas of the heart and personality.

In the Scriptures, we are encouraged to seek God's face. God's face refers to His holy, intimate Presence manifested to humans on earth. In the ultimate sense, we cannot experience His full, unrestrained Presence and live to tell about it. Yet He reveals Himself to us to the degree that we have the capacity—because He wants us to know and experience Him, and He created us for this very purpose.

On this side of eternity, God has created us to know Him intimately, even though there are limitations. Someday, all the hindrances and earthly barriers will be gone, and we will realize our ultimate face-to-face encounter—eternity in His holy Presence.

An Intimate Encounter

God's face really speaks of His intimate, manifest Presence. I like to speak of the teaching about God's Presence as His *general* presence, His *indwelling* presence, and His *intimate* presence. Psalm 139 speaks of His general, invisible presence in this world. While unseen, He is present everywhere.

God calls us to an intimate encounter as we pursue Him with all our hearts. In my understanding, to seek His face today means to set our hearts to seek Him in worship with Biblical understanding, submitting completely to the control of His Spirit with a longing to know and enjoy Him more. It's not about rehearsing a quick list of needs with God but seeking Him because of who He is with a passion for a deeper intimacy and experience of His Presence.

The Original Facebook

Facebook was founded by Mark Zuckerberg, a former Harvard student, in 2004. But the original "Facebook" is the Bible. We see various pictures in many places of people desiring intimate connection with God's face. We also see their angst when something prevents them from experiencing the intimacy and benefits of His face.

The Old Testament followers spoke of God "hiding His face" or even setting His face against people. This reflected those times when His intimate Presence and favor was hindered because of sin (Deuteronomy 32:20; Job 34:29; Psalm 13:1; 30:7; 143:7; Isaiah 54:8; Jeremiah 33:5; Ezekiel 39:23–24; Micah 3:4).

The writers of the Psalms prayed earnestly during those times when God's face was hidden. These were seasons of great distress. They felt fear of being overtaken by their enemies (Psalm 13:1–2), emotionally troubled, and even close to death (104:29; 143:7). As a result, the writers cried out for a restoration of intimacy and favor. Similarly, we are desperate for a life-giving encounter with the face of our Creator and Heavenly Father.

God's Invitation

The Scriptures are clear that God desires that His people know and enjoy Him. He is ready and responsive to restore His people, if they will again seek His face (2 Chronicles 7:14). God wants His children to know the blessing of seeking His face along with the intimacy and favor that comes with it: "Seek the Lord and His strength; seek His face evermore!" (1 Chronicles 16:11; Psalm 105:4). The blessings of seeking His face are also reflected in Psalm 4:6–8.

Psalm 67 reflects on the many ways God blessed Israel so they could be a blessing to the nations. At the source of all these blessings is this vital recognition: "God be merciful to us and bless us, and cause His face to shine upon us" (v. 1). We need His face to shine upon, bless, and envelop us—because all that we are and all that we do in obedience to His commands and commission is the overflow of intimacy and the fruit of His blessing.

The Divine Initiative

There are countless stories, in Scripture and in history, of people who were blessed and changed by a face-to-face encounter with God. Tomorrow, we will unpack numerous examples. But this book isn't about them. It's about us.

Here's the good news: The invitation to seek His face is offered to you, right now. I love the divine initiative of Psalm 27:8: "When You said, 'Seek My face,' my heart said to You, 'Your face, Lord, I will seek.' " He is saying to us, "Seek My face." Now we must hear the call—and answer.

One of the greatest expressions of God's heart is found in the well-known Aaronic blessing. It was the benediction pronounced by the priest after every morning and evening sacrifice with uplifted hands. It was also the blessing regularly pronounced at the close of all services in the synagogues. The people always responded to it with a united "Amen":

The Lord bless you and keep you;

The Lord make His face shine upon you,

And be gracious to you;

The Lord lift up His countenance upon you,

And give you peace.

NUMBERS 6:24–26

Face time with the Almighty was the key to blessing, protection, grace, and peace. It is still true today. Let us join our voices and say, "Amen!"

Join us in prayer for Day 4
at www.strategicrenewal.com/21days

Face-to-Face – Biblical Encounters with God

With this idea of "Facetime" in mind, let's take some time in to-day's reading to look at some profound Biblical examples. In both the Old and New Testaments, we find accounts of individuals blessed and changed by an encounter with God's face.

Old Testament Encounters

• Abraham encountered the presence of Almighty God and fell on his face in humble worship (Genesis 17:3). God's covenantal blessing and the promise of a son emerged from this encounter.

• Moses spoke to the Lord "face to face, as a man speaks to his friend." He taught Joshua to do the same (Exodus 33:11–12). The mark of their lives and leadership is that the Lord was with them (Joshua 1:17; 3:7). They sought His face and manifested His Presence. Still, Moses experienced a unique intimacy. At the time of his death, it was noted, "But since then there has not arisen in Israel a prophet like Moses, whom the Lord knew face to face" (Deuteronomy 34:10).

• Gideon's military exploits included a moment when he encountered the Angel of the Lord, receiving the assurance of peace and the promise of God's powerful Presence. In response, he declares, "Alas, O Lord God! For I have seen the Angel of the Lord face to face" (Judges 6:22). Confidence and courage came when this leader encountered God.

• David wrote compellingly of his experience of seeking God's face. In Psalm 17:15, he said, "As for me, I will see Your face in righteousness; I shall be satisfied when I awake in Your likeness." He described true worshipers, walking in God's blessing, as "the generation of those who seek Him, who seek Your face" (Psalm 24:6). In Psalm 27:4, he resolved that his one desire was to experience God's Presence and behold the beauty of the Lord. In the midst of persecution and perplexity, David wrote, "Make Your face shine upon Your servant; save me for Your mercies' sake" (Psalm 31:16). He knew that face-to-face intimacy was the secret to his integrity and his wisdom (Psalm 41:12; 119:135).

When that intimacy was interrupted, David knew it. In Psalm 30:7, he wrote, "By Your favor You have made my mountain stand strong; You hid Your face, and I was troubled." Again, in Psalm 27:9, he prayed, "Do not hide Your face from me; do not turn Your servant away in anger; You have been my help; do not leave me nor forsake me, O God of my salvation." We see his great prayer of confession, where he recognized his violation of God's holy Presence: "Hide Your face from my sins, and blot out all my iniquities" (Psalm 51:9). David was a man after God's own heart—and he understood what it meant to seek His face.

• Job—a man of great integrity, patience, and endurance— was tested severely by God in almost every category of his life. During his personal audience with Almighty God, Job learned the core lesson of his encounter. In response, Job prayed, "I have heard of You by the hearing of the ear, but now my eye sees You. Therefore I abhor myself, and repent in dust and ashes" (Job 42:5–6). Face to face, Job became aware of the deep issues of his heart, repented, and went to the next level in his intimacy with the Almighty. Blessings followed.

• Isaiah saw the Lord high and lifted up, surrounded by seraphim and radiant in His holiness (Isaiah 6:1–8). This face-to-face encounter drove him to cry out in confession, "Woe is me, for I am undone!" From that awesome moment of worship, confession, and cleansing, Isaiah received his call and responded, "Here am I! Send me." When we seek His face, we are cleansed, changed, and called into vital service for His kingdom.

New Testament Encounters

• Thomas saw the faith and hope of his colleagues after their gathering with the risen Christ. Thomas was not among them in their initial encounter. Days later, he "saw for himself" as Jesus again appeared. Addressing Thomas directly, the Lord told Thomas to reach out and touch His wounds, but all Thomas needed to do was see Jesus and he was transformed from doubt to bold declaration, proclaiming Jesus as his Lord and God (John 20:28).

• Paul was on a road trip hunting down the "people of the way," who were multiplying like rabbits and posing a threat to the Jewish religious system. At the instant he met the risen Lord face-to-face, he fell to the ground. In the days following, he was physically blind but captivated with the face of Christ as he prayed on Straight Street (Acts 9:11). His hunger grew so much that he spent three years on the backside of a desert, seeking Christ and learning from Him. Face time turned Paul into the greatest missionary the world has ever known.

• John, the elderly apostle, was banished on the Isle of Patmos. As he worshiped on the Lord's Day, he encountered a powerful face-to-face moment with the risen Jesus. He described Christ's face with these words: "His head and hair were white like wool, as white as snow, and His eyes like a flame of fire.... His voice as the sound of many waters... and His countenance was like the sun shining in its strength" (Revelation 1:14–16). And what did John do? He writes, "And when I saw Him, I fell at His feet as dead. But He laid His right hand on me, saying to me, 'Do not be afraid; I am the First and the Last. I am He who lives, and was dead, and behold, I am alive for-evermore. Amen. And I have the keys of Hades and of Death'" (Revelation 1:17–18).

This is the Christ whose face we seek. How can we be content with anything less when we consider the privilege of prayer? How can we remain the same when we encounter the living God in authentic intimacy?

Join us in prayer for Day 5
at www.strategicrenewal.com/21days

Glowin' Moses
and a Transformed You

When I was a boy, my parents and I would visit my older brother and his new wife in Missouri, where they attended Bible college. My fondest memory of those trips can be summarized in one word: fireflies. At dusk, no one needed to ask where I was. Chasing those flashing fluorescent-green insects captivated my imagination.

Scientists say that the luminosity of these little guys occurs when the enzyme luciferase acts on luciferin in the presence of magnesium ion, ATP (adenosine triphosphate), and oxygen to produce light.[1] There's a Bible story of a luminous creature that stands above them all. I call it *The Chronicle of Glowin' Moses*. The explanation of his brightness is not chemical but miraculous and captivating.

Reflecting a Holy Presence

Let us go back about thirty-five hundred years to a scene described in Exodus 34:29–35. Moses had just spent his second forty days on the holy mountain, meeting with God, receiving the Law from the Almighty.

Moses met with God in intimate interchange and descended the mountain. With a second copy of the Ten Commandments in hand, Moses arrived in camp—GLOWING! God's Presence was so real that it left its mark on Moses' face. The brightness was so overwhelming that it frightened the people. Moses had to put a veil over his face. Every time he went back to meet with God, experiencing His intimate Presence and receiving His truth for the people, Moses would remove the veil in unhindered divine fellowship. Moses knew the glory of God's Presence, open-faced—only to return to speak to the people with the protection of the veil.

Experiencing the Glory

With that inspiration in mind, stay with me because this story of Moses' glow and glory culminates in your prayer life. Let's fast-forward fifteen hundred years, from Moses to approximately AD 55. Here we find Paul comparing the scenario of Moses' Old Testament glory-glow with our own New Testament experience of the Presence of Christ (2 Corinthians 3:1–4:6). Paul says that Moses' radiance was a temporary, fading exhibit of the lesser and passing power of the Law, written on stone, and ultimately bringing condemnation because of our sin. Conversely, His Spirit has called us into a new agreement with God, with truth written on our hearts, not on slabs of rock. Because of Christ, we are made righteous and now experience a glory far beyond the slow-fading glow of Moses. The glory is within us now. It is not found in a law or temple but in the face of Jesus, who, through His indwelling Presence, invites us into an intimate encounter with Himself.

When it comes to our access to the throne of Christ's grace, Paul writes, "But we all, with unveiled face, beholding as in a mirror the glory of the Lord, are being transformed" (2 Corinthians 3:18). Every believer now has the privilege of "beholding" through an intimate encounter with the glory (Presence and person) of Jesus Christ. We can enjoy this reality individually and collectively every time we pray.

The Power to Become

So, what is the result? Paul says that we "are being transformed into the same image from glory to glory, just as by the Spirit of the Lord" (2 Corinthians 3:18). Yes, God uses prayer to change things. Yet at the core of Paul's theology of life and ministry is this amazing truth that communion with Christ changes us! This is no superficial rearranging of the activities, approaches, and attitudes of life. This is inside-out change. Transformation.

The English pronunciation of this Greek word is *metamourfoumetha*—very similar to our idea of a metamorphosis. It is the same word used to describe the transfiguration of Christ (Matthew 17:2), and in Romans 12:2, we are similarly challenged to be "transformed by the renewing of your mind." This is a progressive, continuous change of heart and character from one level of glory to another. To change from "glory to glory" really speaks of an ever-advancing life of Christ-centered focus and Christlike fruitfulness. This all occurs by the power of the indwelling Spirit of Christ in our lives. We are captivated by Christ, changed by Christ, and conformed to Christ.

First Encounter!

This idea of transforming prayer was more than theory to Paul. He had been looking for glory in the Old Covenant. As you know, everything changed for Paul (formerly Saul) one day on the dirt road to Damascus when the living Christ appeared in radiance and drove Paul to his face.

We do not know with certainty what Paul prayed about for those three days when he was blind and fasting. We know his heart was immediately touched on that Damascus road with a desire to know Christ and His will for Paul's life. We do know that in the course of all of his writings, Paul never requested prayer for an arthritic knee, hair loss, or quick healing of his many back wounds inflicted by his persecutors. He often prayed for a greater knowledge of Jesus, a deeper joy in suffering, a fuller experience of His love, an enduring boldness in preaching Christ, and an ultimate revelation of His glory (Philippians 1:19–26; 3:10; Ephesians 3:14–19; 6:19–20).

Time to Go for the Glory

Fireflies are entertaining. Glowin' Moses was truly amazing. Paul was changed in a moment. Still, there is nothing so attractive and captivating in this sin-darkened world as a Christian who experiences and exhibits the glory of Jesus through the power of face-to-face intimacy.

Now it is time to understand the core truths and practices that make prayer so transformational. It's time to go for the glory.

Join us in prayer for Day 6
at www.strategicrenewal.com/21days

The Case of the Missing Prayer List

Let's talk about best practices... not good, not acceptable, not traditional, not comfortable, not common practices—but the best. That is the passion of the next few days. My prayer is that these ideas and ideals will inspire you to something very Biblical, fresh, practical, and transforming in your prayer life.

In relation to prayer, we want to use all we know from the Scriptures to discover the best practices. We want to learn to understand the leading of the Spirit to experience and achieve the desired result—the glory of God (we will talk more about this "desired result" as you continue to read). This would be "best-practices praying."

We need to thoroughly know and understand what it means to seek God's face in worship-based prayer. We need the Spirit to give us holy dissatisfaction and the motivation to change. We need to know how to engage in transforming prayer.

No Prayer Leftovers

To realize best-practices prayer, we must take an honest look at where we are. Good things are taking place in the lives of many Christians. Churches are making noble attempts to pray. Yet we all want God's best, which I believe is clear in the Scriptures and within reach of every true believer.

Unfortunately, we seem to give God our spiritual leftovers in prayer. If you were celebrating your tenth wedding anniversary and wanted it to be the best it could be, you would not announce to your spouse, "We are going to stay home and have leftovers."

Similarly, when we engage in the great privilege and joy of prayer with a "leftovers mentality," the likelihood of spiritual blessing is slight. The Lord says, "Love me with all of your heart," worship me "in spirit and in truth," present your bodies as a "living sacrifice." He calls for our passionate best. Instead, we bring spiritual leftovers to the throne of grace. This is not a best practice. Far from it.

Quality Not Quantity

In Malachi 1, God addressed this attitude of spiritual leftovers, which had become acceptable in the worship routines of Israel. The Lord did not require great quantities—but He did ask for their first and best as a demonstration of their gratitude to God as the source of all their blessings and an indication of their reverence for God as the One worthy of worship.

Instead, they were bringing leftovers. They offered blind, lame, and sick animals to God at the Temple. The priests were conducting good services. The people were going through the motions. On the surface, all looked well. Yet in Malachi 1:6, we find, "'Where is My honor? And if I am a Master, where is My reverence?' says the Lord of hosts to you priests who despise My name."

Acceptable Sacrifices

Today, we are far removed from that scene in Jerusalem. Christ has become our atoning sacrifice, so we no longer need animals or grain to sacrifice. Yet our gratitude to and reverence for God in prayer and worship should continue.

From a New Testament standpoint, acceptable sacrifices include:

- A commitment to worship in spirit and in truth (John 4:22–24)

- A genuine sacrifice of praise, giving thanks to His name (Hebrews 13:15)

- The presentation of our bodies in complete surrender (Romans 12:1–2)

- A life of love that produces right living (Philippians 1:9–11)

- Doing everything "in the name of the Lord Jesus" with thanksgiving (Colossians 3:17)

- Service conducted in supernatural power (1 Peter 4:11)

- Generosity that flows from a heart of love (Philippians 4:10–19)

Relating to prayer, God is not looking for a dutiful contribution of time or energy in the spirit of religious observance. He is looking for a hungry heart that seeks after Him in praise, gratitude, and loving surrender with a readiness to pray, think, and live like Jesus as the expression and overflow of that intimacy.

Rethinking Our Lists

I have to admit, I have never been much of a prayer-list person. But for some people, lists and guides can be very helpful. Lists can help us remember things for which we should pray. They help us track answers to prayer. They can help us remember details such as names, ministry issues, dates, and elements of spiritual progress in situations and lives. Lists can prevent our minds from wandering in prayer. Perhaps when it comes to journaling and managing lists, we are safe to conclude "to each his own."

Yet in group settings, the focus on lists of needs and prolonged discussions about details can distract from the purpose. Some groups spend significant time talking and taking notes about issues, people, and problems. Those discussions can border on gossip. This is not a best practice. Additionally, we can tend to operate simply in the realm of our own human thoughts, our own observations, and our own ideas concerning what we should pray about. We often ask the question, "What do we need to pray about?" instead of actually praying.

What's the Big Deal?

So, you are probably thinking, *Come on, Henderson, what's the big deal? At least folks are trying to keep track of things in their prayer lives! Be grateful people are getting together to pray.* Yes, praise God for faithful, praying people. However, this section is about best-practices praying—and we all know that being stuck in a rut of practicing good things can become a hindrance to the practice of the best things.

To be honest, I find little evidence in the Bible for our routine emphasis on extensive prayer lists focused almost entirely on temporal concerns.[1] I don't want to be legalistic, but I do want to jolt us out of a rut of thinking that lists are the key to effective prayers.

Lists are simply tools. I am not suggesting that everyone stop using prayer lists. But we must recognize the possibility that our prayer lists are replacing the Scriptures and the Spirit as the primary content providers for our prayer times. We want to keep pursuing best practices that meet the goal of God's glory. Again, we must embrace prayer as transformational, not merely utilitarian.

Join us in prayer for Day 7
at www.strategicrenewal.com/21days

All Prayer Requests
Are Not Created Equal

Asking is a vital component of our relationship with God. This is true because He has commanded us to seek Him as our ultimate source in all things. He has ordained prayer as the means by which we depend on and trust in Him. He answers our prayers to give us what He knows we need to bring Him glory.

Like anyone, I love it when God answers my prayers in ways that make my life more pleasant or pain-free. Yet I am learning that my deepest needs are met when my heart is most closely aligned with the Word of God, the Son of God, the Spirit of God, and the purposes of God. I feel God calling me beyond superficial solutions as the focus of my prayers to discovering the profound joy of a transformed life.

Our Father knows, cares, and is fully capable of taking care of all our needs according to His will and glory. Yet the privilege of prayer offers so much more.

Birds, Lilies, and the Kingdom

In Matthew chapter 6, Jesus preaches the importance of pure motives in our giving, praying, and fasting. He warns against materialism. He provides a powerful antidote for worry by illustrating His care for the birds of the sky and the flowers of the field.

In considering these truths, we must search our souls concerning the things that trigger our prayers. What values shape our requests? Are our motives honoring to Christ? To what degree are "earthly treasures" and the "god of mammon" infecting our prayer life? Amid all our worries regarding our health, finances, family, job, education, and ministry concerns, are we seeking first His kingdom and not our own?

Toward Spontaneity and Substance

Two vital concerns emerge here. First is the need to allow the good gift of the Spirit to lead us in the freedom to pray His heart, not our predetermined ideas. The second issue is the need to align our attitude and approach with the patterns of the Scriptures when we are praying about issues and needs. God continues to teach me so many amazing lessons about the need for spiritual spontaneity over routine rehearsals of prayer lists. He keeps calling me to align my prayers more completely with the precepts, priorities, and patterns of Scripture.

We know we are supposed to bring our requests to God. Yet one of the most important questions we need to ask is how the content of our prayers differ from the Biblical patterns and teaching regarding the things we should be praying about. I suggest that the prayer requests we find in the Bible are shorter, deeper, and fundamentally different in nature than the lists that can tend to dominate the prayer approach of modern Christians.

Praying Just Like Jesus?

Scripture records numerous examples of Jesus' prayer life. We find six references to Jesus' prayers that give no clear indication of the content of what He said (Mark 1:35; 6:46; Luke 3:21; 9:18, 28; 11:1). We find He often withdrew from activity in order to enjoy private communion with the Father. While we do not know the substance of His prayers in these times, it appears they were directly related to fresh empowerment for His self-less, sacrificial service. There are also occasions when Jesus blesses people, but His exact words are not given (Mark 10:16; Luke 24:50).

Jesus' prayer life was distinguished by intimate expressions of worship, thanksgiving, surrender, and gracious intercession for the faith of others. Many modern-day teachers encourage us to "do" like Jesus, lead like Jesus, and speak like Jesus. Our passion must also be to embrace these truths so we can pray like Jesus.

Redirected Disciples

During Jesus' earthly ministry, the disciples were in constant physical interaction with Him, so in many ways, their very conversations were prayers. When it came to specific instances of prayer, they admitted their desire and need to learn (Luke 11:1). Typically, their prayers were selfish and sleepy. They jockeyed for prominence in their requests to Jesus, wanted to call down fire on those who rejected their message, and often doubted.

However, after the Spirit came to permanently indwell them at Pentecost, their prayers changed. John Franklin describes it: "They went from being on their own agenda to being on God's agenda. They quit seeking a seat on Jesus' right and His left and began praying for boldness to testify in the face of persecution. They quit flirting with a return to fishing and focused on shepherding the people of God. They stopped worrying about their circumstances and began seeking an endowment of power from on high to preach the gospel. They changed from being self-centered to being God-centered. This determined their power with God—or rather His power through them." [1]

Paul's Prayer Points

The New Testament contains the specific prayers of the Apostle Paul, offered as he wrote his inspired letters. To see a snapshot of his prayer lists, read the following verses: 1 Thessalonians 3:9–13; 2 Thessalonians 1:3–12; Ephesians 1:3–23; Ephesians 3:14–21; Philippians 1:3–11; Colossians 1:3–14.

Every one of Paul's model prayers sprang from expressions of thanksgiving, truths about God, and notes of praise. They are the fruit of his worship and intimate, experiential knowledge of the person of Christ. Paul's requests were focused on the growing faith and love of believers with the goal of God's glory.

In light of our sometimes significant, sometimes silly patterns, we should look to the Bible to review the occasions when Paul asked for prayer, as we will do in tomorrow's reading. This can also give us some vital guidance about our own requests for prayer. A summary review of Paul's specific personal prayer requests reveals a consistent focus on the advancement of the Gospel message, the fulfillment of the mission, and the ultimate glory of God in all things.

So, what's on your prayer list? Perhaps the fundamental difference between our prayer lists and the prayer concerns we find in the Bible is that we pray about personal problems, while most of the Biblical prayers focus on Christ's purposes. Worship-based prayers set the foundation for something other than "me" prayers because they start with a "Thee" focus. This changes the nature of how we pray.

Join us in prayer for Day 8
at www.strategicrenewal.com/21days

The God-Glorifying Prayers
of Jesus and Paul

Because it is so important to understand the Biblical purposes and patterns of prayer, let's take time today to dig deeper into understanding the New Testament models of prayer.

How Jesus Prayed

• Matthew 11:25—He thanked the Father for His pleasure in hiding truth from some and revealing it to others.

• John 11:41–42—Jesus publicly thanks the Father that He hears His prayers so that others will believe the Father sent Him.

• John 12:27–28—Jesus openly acknowledges His troubled soul in light of His impending sacrifice on the cross but affirms His commitment to the purpose of His coming to earth, declaring, "Father, glorify Your name."

• John 17—In His high priestly prayer, Jesus reflects on the finished task of bringing glory to the Father through His earthly ministry, while asking for the spiritual preservation and unity of His followers for the sake of convincing the unbelieving world that the Father has sent the Son.

• Luke 22:31–32—Jesus prays for Peter that his faith will not fail "as Satan sifts him like wheat" so that in time, Peter will return to Christ and strengthen the faith of others.

• Matthew 26:39, 42; Mark 14:36; Luke 22:42—Jesus prays to the Father, desiring that the "cup of suffering" pass from Him but declaring, "Not as I will, but as You will."

While suffering on the cross, Jesus prays to the Father three times. First, "Father, forgive them, for they do not know what they do" (Luke 23:34), an amazing prayer of mercy and grace. Second, "My God, My God, why have You forsaken Me?" (Matthew 27:46; Mark 15:34), revealing the weight of the condemnation of sin that Jesus bore on our behalf. Third, "Father, into Your hands I commit My spirit" (Luke 23:46), in which Jesus willingly offers Himself in death, as He completes the atoning work.

Paul's Prayer Requests

In 2 Corinthians 1:9–11, we see that the Corinthians had been praying for Paul as he faced death in Asia Minor. We do not know exactly what they prayed, but we do know that Paul was delivered from this life-threatening trial and from self-reliance. The result was a greater faith in Christ and united thanksgiving to God.

In Romans 15:30–33, Paul asks the believers in Rome to strive together with him in prayer because of their regard for Christ and the Spirit's love in their hearts. He specifically requests prayer for protection from the enemies of the Gospel, blessing in the delivery of his love offering to the suffering church in Jerusalem, and God's will in bringing him joyfully to Rome, where he hopes to find refreshing rest in their company.

In considering Paul's desire for deliverance, it is insightful to think about his conversation with the Ephesian elders, which occurred while he was on this very journey to Jerusalem, then to Rome. In Acts 20:23–24, it seems his sole desire for deliverance and survival was for the singular purpose of the Gospel, not his own comfort or avoidance of suffering.

In Ephesians 6:19, Paul adds a personal postscript to his great teaching on spiritual warfare by asking for prayer. He asks them to pray "that utterance may be given to me, that I may open my mouth boldly to make known the mystery of the Gospel." He wrote this from prison but made no mention of a painful trial or his need for a vacation.

In Philippians 1:19, Paul writes again from prison. He asks that they would pray that the Spirit of Jesus Christ would provide his deliverance. Yet in the context, he is content with either deliverance to death and his eternal reward—or a deliverance *from* death and the continuation of his responsibilities of serving others through the Gospel. He wrote clearly about his motive for receiving these prayers when he spoke of his ultimate desire that "Christ will be magnified in my body, whether by life or by death" (Philippians 1:20).

Still writing from prison, Paul asks the fellow believers in Colossae to pray for him, "that God would open to us a door for the word, to speak the mystery of Christ, for which I am also in chains, that I may make it manifest, as I ought to speak" (Colossians 4:3–4). The passionate apostle seemed unconcerned about comfort or survival. He just wanted to fulfill the Gospel purpose of his life.

The Bible and God's Glory

It is clear from Scripture that Christ saves us for God's glory and sets us apart to Himself for His glory.

Writing about "our Lord Jesus Christ, who gave Himself for our sins, that He might deliver us from this present evil age, according to the will of our God and Father," Paul exclaims, "to whom be *glory* forever and ever. Amen" (Galatians 1:3–5). To the Ephesians, Paul speaks of our God's amazing grace in Christ through our election, adoption, and forgiveness—"to the praise of the *glory* of His grace" (Ephesians 1:6), "to the praise of His *glory*" (v. 12), and again, "to the praise of His *glory*" (v. 14).

Second Corinthians 5:15 exclaims that "He died for all, that those who live should live no longer for themselves, but for Him who died for them and rose again." Because we were "bought at a price" we are compelled to "*glorify* God in [our] body and in [our] spirit, which are God's" (1 Corinthians 6:20).

Now, in light of the price He paid, we must pray for the goal of His glory—embracing the full purpose of our salvation.

Set Apart for His Glory

We are being set apart to God and made more like Jesus. Why? For His glory.

The Apostle Peter reminds us that our faith is sometimes tested by fire so that our lives "may be found to praise, honor, and *glory* at the revelation of Jesus Christ" (1 Peter 1:7). He reminds us to serve in the power God provides "that in all things God may be *glorified* through Jesus Christ, to whom belong the *glory* and the dominion forever and ever" (1 Peter 4:11). He concludes his letter with the as-surance that "the God of all grace, who called us to His eternal *glory* by Christ Jesus, after you have suffered a while, perfect, establish, strengthen, and settle you" for the ultimate goal: "To Him be the *glory* and the dominion forever and ever. Amen" (1 Peter 5:10–11).

Jude, the half-brother of Jesus, reassures us with these words: "Now to Him who is able to keep you from stumbling, and to pres-ent you faultless before the presence of His *glory* with exceeding joy, to God our Savior, who alone is wise, be *glory* and majesty, dominion and power, both now and forever. Amen" (Jude 24–25). He sets us apart and keeps us in His grace—for His glory.

Go for the Glory!

Prayer becomes transformational when we embrace the original and enduring context for all praying. A worship-based approach fixes our heart first on the majesty of God, the the person of Christ, the purity of His Word—and excites within us an appetite for Him. Our very motives for prayer are changed and elevated beyond anything merely earthly. Our heart is renewed with a longing for His glory.

Let God Be Magnified

Prayer is about seeking God, rejoicing in Him, and continually focusing on His glory. However, many of us fail to focus our prayers on the core motive: that God would be magnified in everything we seek or say. If we were to be honest, our prayers are often motivated by a desire for comfort and convenience. Many times, our prayers are viewed as a divinely ordained way to get what we want out of life, or to avoid what we don't want. It is easy to fall into the trap of thinking prayer exists so God can be used to help us preserve our glory rather than our being used to promote His glory.

When we understand the ultimate reason for prayer, our asking is no longer aimless. Our "crying out" has deeper conviction. Our prayers for miracles rise fervently because we know God can heal, or heal us of the desire to be healed—all for His glory. Our intercession looks beyond temporal needs and targets transcendent realities that have eternal significance, for His glory.

What Motivates God?

I've heard it said that the only thing that motivates God is His own glory. To our tiny minds that may sound egotistical, but we must remember that God is the Creator and the One to whom glory is due in the purity and beauty of His holiness. He deserves it.

I am motivated by so many lesser things, even in my prayer life, perhaps especially in my prayer life. God's glory should be our sole—and soul—motivation that frames and filters everything we pray. In John 14:13, Jesus gave us a standard for all of our praying, "And whatever you ask in My name, that I will do, that the Father may be *glorified* in the Son." What motivates us to ask can often be all over the map. What motivates our Father to answer is that He would be *glorified* in our prayers through the person and work of His Son, Jesus Christ.

Christ's Work in Us for His Glory

The ultimate result of God's salvation plan is that every knee should bow and every tongue should confess "that Jesus Christ is Lord, to the *glory* of God the Father" (Philippians 2:10–11). Jesus came, lived, loved, served, sacrificed, died, and rose again—for God's glory.

Prayer is the core of our relationship with Christ. This relationship into which we have been called, through the grace of Jesus, exists for God's glory. Christ has saved us for God's glory and is setting us apart to Himself for His glory. With fresh conviction and passion, we can embrace the truth of 1 Corinthians 10:31, where it tells us, "Whether you eat or drink, or whatever you do [including prayer]—do all to the *glory* of God."

Inspiring as these reminders are, our flesh struggles to pray in alignment with the truth of God's glory. Our prayer lists can easily become so saturated with our desires for ease, comfort, convenience, and accomplishment that the goal of God's glory becomes obscured. Our human tendency to avoid pain, loss, and difficulty can dilute our passion for God's glory. When our goals and God's glory are in conflict, it can be hard for our hearts to choose.

Following Jesus to Glory

In John 21:12–17, the resurrected Jesus had appeared to His disciples on the shores of the Sea of Galilee. Jesus interrogated Peter about his love for the Savior, with the thrice-repeated command, "Feed My sheep." Then He makes this fascinating statement: "Most assuredly, I say to you, when you were younger, you girded yourself and walked where you wished; but when you are old, you will stretch out your hands, and another will gird you and carry you where you do not wish" (v. 18). The writer, John, comments, "This He spoke, signifying by what death he would glorify God" (v. 19).

Think about this exchange. Jesus describes a very undesirable death as part of Peter's destiny as an obedient disciple. If we could rate our old age or death scenarios, what Jesus described here is "dreadful." Yet John says it is a death that will glorify God.

As many of us would have done, Peter apparently struggled with this revelation. But Peter also had a deep assurance in the Lord's promise to get him through the "bad" times (1 Peter 5:10–11). Even more remarkable is his strong reminder that we are called to His glory and that it all will culminate in His glory.

Winning the Struggle

So, let's just settle it. Praying for God's glory is a real, daily struggle. But it is the struggle that can and must be won every day. Our transformation and triumph depend on it.

There is a sense that every day, we live with one hand on the perishables of this life: family, health, job, home, hobbies, plans, etc.

In the other hand, we grasp the unseen and eternal reality of think-ing, feeling, speaking, acting, and praying, all for God's glory. Our heart has to choose every day to let go of one to grasp fully the other, with both hands—the entirety of our will and personality.

But we are not alone in the struggle. Early in his journey of loss, pain, and interpersonal attack, Job said the right words and struggled to do the right thing. In the end, he realized that he needed a deeper revelation of God in order to comprehend His glory (Job 42:1–6). Perhaps there is no greater comfort than knowing that the Lord Jesus is our High Priest who can "sympathize with our weak-nesses" because He "was in all points tempted as we are, yet without sin" (Hebrews 4:15).

Thankfully, God gives us grace to "go for the glory." I define *grace* as God doing for us, in us, and through us what only He can do through the person, power, and Presence of Jesus Christ. I have learned that God has tailor-made grace for everything we face. I need the grace to long and pray for His glory.

Join us in prayer for Day 10
at www.strategicrenewal.com/21days

How Abiding Guides Our Asking

After a dynamic, young pastor experienced worship-based prayer, this is the testimony he shared: "It has helped me to see that the ultimate aim of my time with the Lord or with others before the Lord is worship. It is the starting point and the goal."

God's Voice–Our Ear

It is so easy in our perfunctory approach to prayer to blow into God's Presence, conduct our daily data dump to be relieved of our worries but not revived in our worship. Calvin Miller explains, "Too often, we go into God's presence with a list of pleas, trying to talk God into granting our desire. But this kind of praying makes us 'one big mouth' and God 'one grand ear.' But when we pray the Scriptures, it makes God the voice and leaves us as the ear. In short, God gets His turn at getting a word in edgewise."[1]

One core focus of worship-based prayer is the commitment to always start our prayers from the Word of God. This is the key to abiding. Jesus emphasized, "If you abide in Me, and My Words abide in you, you will ask what you desire, and it shall be done for you. By this My Father is glorified, that you bear much fruit; so you will be My disciples" (John 15:7–8).

Abiding and Abundance

The word *abide* means to "continue, remain, dwell, or stay." It is the idea of a life-giving connection with Christ that produces His character and accomplishes His will in us. As Charles Spurgeon noted, *abiding* means "yielding ourselves up to Him to receive His life and to let that life work out its results in us. We live *in* Him, *by* Him, *for* Him, *to* Him when we abide in Him."[2] My friend Bud McCord speaks of abiding in this way: "Jesus in us is the perfection we need to live the Christian life on a moment-by-moment basis."[3] Jesus in us is the perfection we must have to pray.

If prayer is to be more than lists and the language of human reason, we must grasp this command, making the worship-focused relationship with Christ our first desire. Then His Word in us can shape all that we are—and all that we think, especially in prayer. When this happens, our prayers are transformed and so are we.

Clearly, this is the idea of a truth-based intimacy that shapes our prayers and forms the proper expression of our needs. Again, prayer is not just a casual recitation of whatever pains and problems pop into our minds on any given occasion. It is the overflow of a heart focused on the conscious Presence of Christ, clinging to Him and His Word as the source and scope of our lives.

Praying With an Open Bible

While it was not always this way, all of my praying in the last two decades, both personal and in community, has begun with an open Bible. I take time to allow Scripture to speak deeply to my heart and formulate my prayers in response. This sense of Christ's Presence and the substance of His Word guide my heart and mind. When I miss a day of this kind of praying, which is more often than I wish, I feel the difference and the distance.

Speaking about this very idea, John Piper says, "I have seen that those whose prayers are most saturated with Scripture are generally most fervent and most effective in prayer. And where the mind isn't brimming with the Bible, the heart is not generally brimming with prayer."[4] When we do not begin our prayers from this posture of abiding, allowing the Word to saturate our minds and guide our words, our prayers can become short, superficial, shallow, and even selfish.

Praying on the Same Page

A worship-based focus on the face of Christ and His Word is a powerful approach to group prayer, as well. Since 1994, I have known the deep joy of leading a variety of prayer summits every year. These multi-day gatherings have no agenda, speakers, or special music. Those who have never participated in an experience like this wonder what we do to fill the time. In reality, these retreats could be labeled "Word summits" because the vast majority of our praying springs from massive doses of spontaneous Scripture reading offered by any participant who feels led to read aloud. Because God's Word is such a limitless treasure of truth, with countless applications to the human heart, we never run out of material.

Inevitably, the Holy Spirit weaves these passages together in a cohesive way to direct us into specific themes of prayer. Very often, one single passage grips the heart of an individual and becomes the basis of personal meditation and an eventual life-changing response.

Who Starts the Prayer Conversation?

In a sense, prayer is a continual conversation between our hearts and God's. Nevertheless, when we stop to spend time in focused prayer, it is important to know who should start the conversation. If prayer is simply the discharge of my own will and thoughts, in the hope that I can help God run the universe, then I should start the prayer conversation. On the other hand, if prayer is about my heart becoming intimate and aligned with the heart of the Savior, then I should let Him start the conversation. This is the reality of abiding in Him and letting His words abide in us.

Imagine what a difference it would make if we went straight to the Word of God to hear from Him and then based our prayer time in His wisdom, not ours. Consider what insight and direction we would receive if we asked, in the context of prayer, "Lord, what is on Your heart? What truth does the Holy Spirit want us to pray about?" Yes, many of the same needs would surface, but from a different perspective—God's, not ours. The way we pray about our needs would change. With the faith that comes from the Word of God, and the passion that comes from the indwelling Christ, we would pray differently.

Join us in prayer for Day 11
at www.strategicrenewal.com/21days

DAY 12

How His Spirit
Ignites Our Supplication

If you had unlimited resources and wanted your children to become extremely proficient in their learning, you would hire a tutor. Likewise, our Father, with His unlimited resources, and His commitment to teach us to pray, has given us a supernatural tutor. The Holy Spirit is available to us and resides within us 24/7. Our Father longs for intimacy with us and knows that real prayer is impossible apart from the indwelling Spirit. We are enabled to "worship God in the Spirit, rejoice in Christ Jesus, and have no confidence in the flesh" (Philippians 3:3) through worship-based prayer. The Holy Spirit empowers us to know Christ. Worship-based prayer brings us to a greater sensitivity and surrender to the Holy Spirit. As a result, our prayers become Spirit-fueled. And we are transformed.

Graveyard or Insane Asylum

My friend Jim Cymbala urges Christians toward a vibrant and practical reliance on the Holy Spirit. He strongly notes that when it comes to the person of the Holy Spirit, churches tend to be either cemeteries or insane asylums. Some hardly recognize the Holy Spirit or seek Him at all. Others engage in all kinds of bizarre, extra-Biblical antics, for which the Holy Spirit gets "credit." In our prayers, we want to avoid these extremes but must set our hearts on the very real, powerful, and practical reality of the Holy Spirit.

Not only does Jesus want His house (people) to be characterized by prayer (Mark 11:17), but He wants us to be controlled and empowered by the supernatural reality of His Holy Spirit rather than by human strategies and intellectual prowess.

Word, Spirit, and Worship

We've seen that prayer is best experienced with an open Bible. We read the Biblical text, looking for great truths about God. These truths fuel our worship as we engage in prayer and song, in reverence for His name, character, and works. Our meditation and application of these truths becomes powerful as we open our hearts to the Spirit. These are the essentials of transformation.

Paul describes this dynamic in Colossians 3:16. Even though the context of this experience is in community, the same truth applies individually. God's Word is a stimulus to worship and a tool for worship.

Compare that passage with Ephesians 5:18–20. The parallels between Word and Spirit are obvious. When we are under the control of the Holy Spirit, worship overflows. When we are engaged with the Scriptures, worship abounds.

Praying in the Spirit

What exactly is "praying in the Spirit" and what does it accomplish? Let's start with a definition. Some have reduced "praying in the Spirit" to a certain expression of emotion or the crafting of special language in order to solicit God's blessings. In truth, it is much clearer and deeper than any of these modern notions. Greek scholar Kenneth Wuest noted: "Praying in the Spirit is praying in dependence on the Holy Spirit. It is prayer exercised in the sphere of the Holy Spirit, motivated and empowered by Him."[1]

Pastor John Piper defines it simply: "Praying in the Holy Spirit is to be moved and guided by the Holy Spirit in prayer. We pray by His power and according to His direction."[2] Basically, praying in the Spirit is vital to worship—to knowing God's heart. Then we can pray His agenda with confidence as requests are actually prompted by the Spirit, not the flesh.

In the school of prayer and Christian living, the subject is not simply difficult—it is supernatural. Fortunately, we have a supernatural teacher in the Holy Spirit. The good news is that He speaks clearly, specifically, and helpfully so that we can understand exactly what we need to know and apply from the truth He inspired.

Spirit Scriptures

The Scriptures affirm that the best way to hear from the Spirit is to fill the mind with the Word of God, accompanied by careful reading and meditation on the sacred text. That's the best way to receive what the Spirit is speaking clearly.

Even the Apostle Paul confesses that in our mere human intellect, we are not able to pray effectively. Our minds and hearts are weak. The Holy Spirit moves and prays within us, in perfect harmony with the will of the Father and the Son. The Spirit works in us to tutor us in prayer according to the will of God, as we have assurance of God's goodness and sovereignty in the unfolding of the events of our lives (Romans 8:28). The Spirit works in us to make us like Jesus (v. 29) and to keep transforming us until we are in glory with Him (v. 30).

His Goal—Our Choice.

Every one of us is confronted with a choice. Will we allow familiarity to breed apathy and ineffectiveness as we tune out the vital instructions? Will we be content to simply pray from our own intellectual framework of understanding, with potentially careless and endless lists of ideas that have not been surrendered to the power of the Word and the Spirit? Will we merely seek God's hand to get what we think we need to get by for another week as we hurry in and out of His Presence? Or will we seek His face, from His Word, by His Spirit as we learn to pray in a life-transforming fashion? Jesus promised clear guidance, insight, and a life that brings Him glory. We must take out our earbuds of tradition and apathy and listen. It will change our lives.

Join us in prayer for Day 12
at www.strategicrenewal.com/21days

How His Name Corrects
Our Nonsense

There is no name like the name of Jesus Christ. Knowing the power of His name, most of us remember to tack it on to our prayers virtually every time we pray. However, our traditional reason for remembering His name may be for our own purposes, rather than His.

Truth or Tradition?

Most of us know the idea of praying in Jesus' name is far beyond the routine of adding these three words on the end of a prayer. Yet when we do not do it, we feel almost heretical. It is the traditional thing to do. In group or public prayers, it is a given that whoever prays better wrap it up "in Jesus' name." When they fail to do so, they may get a few raised eyebrows and words of doubt about the spiritual legitimacy of their prayers. After all, will God really hear their prayers if they fail to include this three-word add-on?

One of the amazing benefits of a worship-based approach to prayer is that it fundamentally takes our eyes off ourselves and fixes them on Christ. We establish our prayer experience on Him, not ourselves. We seek to pray His thoughts, not our own.

As the Spirit takes the conductor's wand of the Scriptures and orchestrates our praying, we cannot help but turn our eyes upon

Jesus and "look full in His wonderful face." Then, as the hymn continues, "the things of earth will grow strangely dim in the light of His glory and grace."[1] At that moment of wonder and intimacy, we are really in the place to truly pray in Jesus' name, regardless of the final three words of the prayer.

What's in a Name?

The first formal mention of prayer in the Bible occurs in Genesis 4:26: "Then men began to call on the name of the Lord." The "name of the Lord" represents more than a title for God. It is the essence of His identity and character revealed to the hearts of men. This passage pictures humanity's first response to God's revelation of Himself, crying aloud to Him in prayer. God reveals Himself in His names throughout the Scriptures.

Jesus continued this focus on God's name when He taught His disciples that the first expression of all prayer is "Our Father in Heaven, hallowed be Your *name*" (Matthew 6:9). Christ introduced His followers to a new reality of God as their personal and intimate Father, which would become personal and powerful through His saving work. Jesus taught that prayer is a response to the name of God—which is holy, revered, and worthy of our worship.

My Name Is Jesus, and...

Throughout His ministry, Jesus brought great clarity to us about His character and identity by declaring His unique names. The fullness of God in Christ becomes clear. This is God's gracious work in drawing us to a deeper knowledge of Him and a greater response in prayer. He excited their worship, for example, with the "I am" statements Jesus made in the Gospel of John:

- "I am the bread of life" (John 6:35).
- "I am the light of the world" (John 8:12; 9:5).
- "I am the gate for the sheep" (John 10:7, 9 NIV).

- "I am the good shepherd" (John 10:14).

- "I am the resurrection and the life" (John 11:25).

- "I am the way, the truth, and the life" (John 14:6).

- "I am the true vine" (15:1, 5).

In Jesus' final upper room gathering with His disciples, He taught, "No one comes to the Father except through Me" (John 14:6) and "He who has seen Me has seen the Father" (John 14:9). Because of Jesus' divinity, union with the Father, miraculous works, and supernatural commission He will give to His disciples, He now establishes a profound new normal in prayer. Read carefully: "Most assuredly, I say to you, he who believes in Me, the works that I do he will do also; and greater works than these he will do, because I go to My Father. And whatever you ask in *My name*, that I will do, that the Father may be glorified in the Son. If you ask anything in *My name*, I will do it" (John 14:12–14).

Condition and Result

So, what was Jesus trying to help us understand? Really, He gives us a condition and result for all of our requests. The condition is that we ask in Jesus' name. In his excellent book *The God Who Hears*, W. Bingham Hunter summarizes the New Testament teaching about praying in Jesus' name with these four truths:

- It seeks the glory of God.

- Its foundation is the death, resurrection, and intercession of Jesus.

- It is offered by Jesus' obedient disciples. (Hunter points out that praying in Jesus' name is virtually synonymous with obedience to Jesus.)

- It asks what Jesus Himself would pray for.[2]

Hunter goes on to summarize: "The shortest and perhaps the best answer is simply: Jesus prayed according to the will of God. And that, ultimately, is what it means for you and me to pray in Jesus' name—to pray according to the will of God."[3] This explains why Jesus was so emphatic that *whatever* we ask in *His name*, we will receive. This has also changed the way I start, not just end, my prayers.

Praying in Jesus' Name

What happens when we pray in Jesus' name? What is the ultimate purpose and outcome? According to Jesus' multiple commands in this upper room discourse (John 13–17), the outcomes of praying in His name are:

- The Father will be glorified in the Son.
- We bear fruit that remains.
- Our joy is full.

How many times has prayer frustrated you rather than fulfilled you? Frustration comes from bombarding heaven with our own ideas of what God should do to accomplish our will in Heaven. Fulfillment comes from knowing that His will is being implemented in our lives. Deep reward is found in knowing that the Father is glorified by our prayers and that our relationship with Him is producing the lasting fruit of deep character and spiritual impact. Joy comes from this deep fulfillment.

Jesus' name matters when we converse with Him through prayer. When we get it right, He is honored and we are blessed. The real joy and assurance in prayer comes from the primary focus of seeking Christ's person and Presence prior to His provision. Out of that intimacy of seeking His face, we discover again the wonder of His character, His heart, His purpose, and His will.

How Revelation Motivates Our Response

Have you ever been driving and become so absorbed in music or conversation that you missed your turn and ended up where you never meant to be? Well, I don't want you to miss this turn either!

As we've already noted, worship is the response of all I am to the revelation of all He is. Revelation always requires a response. One of the amazing realities of worship-based prayer is the depth of response it evokes in our souls based on the revelation we pursue in God's Word as the beginning place of prayer. You do not want to miss the turn from all-embracing worship to all-consuming response. This is the elation of life change in the Presence of God.

Don't Miss This Turn!

Indisputably, the book of Romans contains some of the most profound theology of the New Testament. The first eleven chapters of Romans are packed with profound truths about God's saving and sanctifying work in Christ.

Now, don't miss the turn that takes place in chapter 12. If you do, you will not reach your Christ-honoring destination. "I beseech you *therefore*, brethren, by the mercies of God, that you present your bodies a living sacrifice, holy, acceptable to God, which is your reasonable service. And do not be conformed to this world, but be transformed by the renewing of your mind, that you may prove what is that good and acceptable and perfect will of God" (vv. 1–2). The idea is clear. The response to all of this truth—the required acknowledgment of these great expressions of God's character and salvation plan—is sacrificial surrender to God and a renewed commitment to obedience to His will. This is the nature of all real spiritual growth and certainly core to transforming prayer.

In the truest sense, a person cannot pray and remain the same. The commitment to seeking God's face in prayer, when properly understood and faithfully engaged, empowers personal change at the deepest level. I've seen it happen in the hearts of men who pray together from the Scriptures one morning each week. I've observed people receive a call to full-time vocational service in a moment of prayer. I have watched Spirit-prompted reconciliation occur in ways that years of dialog and even counseling could not accomplish.

When anyone is in the presence of something very powerful and unusual to their normal experience, it is difficult to remain the same. Prayer that begins with a pursuit of God's face, an encounter with His character, an experience of His Presence—changes us at the deepest level. We must be aware of the Spirit and the Word working to help us make the turn of transformational response. His worthiness exposes our neediness. I say it all the time: "He is Worthy! I am needy!"

Four common and essential responses are a believing faith, authentic confession, conformity to His will, and empowerment for spiritual warfare.

His Face Evokes Our Faith

Worship-based prayer is a powerful spark that produces a response of faith. When we begin our prayers with a passionate pursuit of the character of God, we are gripped with the reality that "He is" and are soon reminded that "He is a rewarder of those who diligently seek Him." Again, notice the focus on "seeking Him," not just trying to solicit His help or provision. This is an emphasis on His face and a key to faith.

His Character Motivates Our Confession

Another very natural response in the Presence of a holy God is genuine confession of the attitudes, actions, words, and intentions that are inconsistent with His character.

Confession means "agreeing with God" about our sin and failure to align with His person, purpose, and plan. First John 1:9 is so familiar yet empowering: "If we confess our sins, He is faithful and just to forgive us our sins and to cleanse us from all unrighteousness." When a genuine believer walks in the light and truth of Jesus, confession is the normal overflow of the heart.

Our Wonder Leads to His Will

Our Lord and Master has a will. It is the specific and intimate expression of His heart. His Word is His will. The application is revealed by His Spirit. Our requests that have not been surrendered to His Word and Spirit in intimate pursuit may simply reflect our will, not His. Thus, our clarity and confidence about the effect of our prayers will be clouded. Yet when our intent is clear and consecrated—"Your kingdom come, Your will be done"—we have confidence. Knowing His will comes from knowing Him, not just passing a list under His watchful eye.

Our Worship Empowers Our Warfare

Worship-based prayer infuses us with empowerment for the warfare zone we exist in every day of our lives. Word-infused prayer makes us ready to face spiritual enemies with, "It is written" on our lips. Spirit-led prayer allows us to make application of truth to the challenges of the day and weakness of our flesh. We are on the winning team. All the provisions for conquering in life are abundant and available in Christ. Prayer is vital to our daily triumph and awakens us to the necessity of entering battle with a clear mission plan.

I may be naïve compared to the "warfare experts," but I have discovered that a life of passionate worship—one that delights in Biblical truth about God's character, seeks the empowerment of the Spirit for application and articulation, then surrenders in every way as prompted by this intimate encounter, is equipped to "fight the good fight" every day. Jesus, on the heels of forty days of prayer and fasting, wielded the truth of God's Word in facing down the devil in the wilderness (Matthew 4:4–11). We, too, are equipped by His sufficiency to brandish the "sword of the Spirit," which is the spoken Word of God (Ephesians 6:17). We have His perfection and power living in us. He has given us the victory in His finished work of redemption. As we abide in Him, with hearts fully responsive to His intimate revelation of truth and insight, we overcome temptation and are delivered from evil.

Turns Ahead

In the next few days, we will speak very practically about the methodology of worship-based prayer. The promise of transformation is applied when we engage in the reality of seeking God's face. Don't miss the turn. Revelation produces response. Response fuels confession, understanding of God's will, engagement in the battle, and fresh power for the mission. Everything is at stake. Let's proceed together.

Join us in prayer for Day 14
at www.strategicrenewal.com/21days

Pray This, Not That

David Zinczenko was once an overweight child. Today, he is a leading expert on health and fitness, working as editor-in-chief of *Men's Health* magazine and editorial director of *Women's Health* magazine. He is also the author of numerous *New York Times* bestsellers, including a series of books based on his blockbuster hit *Eat This, Not That!*

Every day, millions of people pray in some form or fashion. Every day, Jesus offers the truth and tools to help us do it effectively. In a real sense, He says, "Pray this, not that." His teaching is contained in the all-time bestseller, the Bible, which is the true owner's manual for life. The One who invented prayer tells us how to do it.

In Matthew 6:9–13, the Lord's Prayer, Jesus delivers the all-time final word on how *not to* pray—and how *to* pray. As multitudes flocked to hear Him on the hillside, His words resonated with unparalleled authority and practical application. For over two centuries, this prayer has equipped countless lives for real transformation.

Don't Pray with Impure Motives

Jesus said, "And when you pray, you shall not be like the hypocrites. For they love to pray standing in the synagogues and on the corners of the streets, that they may be seen by men. Assuredly, I say to you, they have their reward" (Matthew 6:5).

When prayer becomes a religious exercise rather than a relational experience, it is formalized and convoluted, as was the case with the Pharisees of Jesus' day. It became a parade of religious stature and, as such, was proudly exhibited before the watching eyes of the adoring followers.

Jesus did not mean here that it is wrong to pray in a group or public setting. He did say that if your motive is to impress people, you'd better enjoy the moment, because that motive did not make the grade for eternal reward. This compelled the disciples to gather in the privacy of an upper room rather than some venue for public consumption.

Don't Pray Using Ineffective Methods

Jesus turned His attention to another misguided group, the Gentiles. These were non-Jewish people, also known as heathen, who did not know, or pray to, the God of Israel. Jesus said of them, "And when you pray, do not use vain repetitions as the heathen do. For they think that they will be heard for their many words" (Matthew 6:7).

At the root of this wrong approach to prayer was a *flawed view of God*. The heathen apparently believed that their god was distant, impressed by religious performance and a bit temperamental in deciding to respond to their prayers. Their gods were in need of the persuasion of human prayers and seemed to require much coercion and repetition to act.

Some people today repeat the Lord's Prayer verbatim as some kind of magical charm. But we understand that prayer is not about a *manipulation of words*. Our Father is completely dialed-in and capable. He is all-knowing and sovereign. He does not need the persuasion of our words or vigorous religious performances in order to know and meet our needs.

Motivational Mistakes

In the next days, we are going to unpack some direct and practical application of the pattern Jesus gave us, showing how we can use it to pray from the Scriptures. First, though, let's examine our own motivations and methods.

As much as we do not like to admit it, it's easy to be caught up in our own religious activities and go through the motions with convoluted motives. Like it or not, we are a performance-oriented society, and the Church is just as bad, if not worse in some ways, as the world.

In my own journey and evaluation, I have concluded that some of our common motives are:

- *Guilt*—the belief that if I do not pray, I will not be an acceptable Christian. Of course, no one wants another person to spend time with him or her simply to avoid or alleviate guilt. The Lord is no different.

- *Approval*—the belief that if I do pray, I will be an acceptable Christian in the eyes of others. This was the flaw of the Pharisees.

- *Church growth*—the belief that prayer can be a useful tool to meet my tangible ministry goals. I know my own tendency to pray so that God will use me—for me. God will not reduce something as pure as prayer to my next ego-driven church-growth tactic.

- *Revival*—the belief that God will bring revival if I will just "work Him" enough through prayer. Of course, we all long for and desperately need revival. A few years ago, I heard a friend say, "There is a difference between seeking revival from God and seeking God for revival."

The Enduring Motive

Graciously, the Lord has taught me that the only enduring motive for prayer is that God is worthy to be sought. Again, this is a worship-based motivation. I may or may not feel like praying. The prayer time may be energized; it may be dull. The answers to prayer may be apparent; they may not. Still, God is worthy to be sought.

So, we pray because God is worthy. But, as we noted already, there is a second side to the motivational coin: I am needy. As I said earlier, prayerlessness is our declaration of independence from God.

He is worthy! We are needy! We must pray with consistency and passion of this rhythm—until we take our last breath.

Adjusting the Approach

As we prepare to clearly understand and apply a pattern that can enliven our prayer life and give us a Biblical, balanced approach to prayer, let's review a quick list of "pray this, not that" principles:

- Pray to seek God's face, NOT just His hand.

- Pray with your heart fixed on God's glory, NOT just for personal satisfaction.

- Pray from the treasury of God's Word, NOT from a list of your own ideas.

- Pray according to the Spirit's instruction, NOT only from human reason.

- Pray with a heart completely surrendered to His will, NOT with a hurried personal agenda.

- Pray in anticipation of living triumphantly in the war zone, NOT in satisfaction with your comfort zone.

- Pray that God would change you, NOT simply change *things*.

I assure you that an approach of worship-based prayer will open new windows of understanding about real intimacy with God. I believe it will empower your life for God's glory and your practical good. Ultimately, you will have to find your own way as you learn to pray by praying.

Join us in prayer for Day 15
at www.strategicrenewal.com/21days

Transforming Prayer
for Dummies

The Lord's Prayer is the ultimate pattern of prayer Jesus gave to His disciples. He repeated it twice in the Gospels. The first delivery (Matthew 6) occurred near Galilee before a large crowd in the context of an extended sermon. His second iteration (Luke 11) occurred near Jerusalem after the disciples observed Him in prayer. He repeated this specific pattern after they made a request to learn how to pray.

In one of the simplest analyses, we find that the Lord's Prayer has two main components.[1] The first section is about God's glory ("Hallowed be Your name. Your kingdom come. Your will be done"). The second part deals with man's need ("Give us day by day our daily bread. Forgive us our sins; do not lead us into temptation" (Luke 11]. Again, this is the heart of all prayer. He is worthy. I am needy. He is my all-sufficient, holy, and sovereign Father. I am His humble, weak, and dependent child. When these two realities meet, prayer transpires.

Today, I am going to share an easy, memorable, and applicable tool you can use at any time to pray the essence of this prayer.

Simple and Applicable

The *FOR DUMMIES* book series is one of the strongest and most instantly identifiable brands in publishing. With more than

200 million books in print and more than 1,600 titles, the "Dummies" books do their best to present often complex subjects in plain English.

The Lord's Prayer is not complex, but a couple decades ago, I discovered a simple way to understand and implement this incredible prayer throughout my prayer life. I call it the "For Dummies" version because is it so simple and immediately applicable—and memorable. It has become a standard approach for my personal prayers.

The 4/4 Pattern

I grew up with a love for music. I played a couple of instruments, sang in high school all-state choirs, and received a scholarship for vocal music for two of my four years of college. So, it was natural that I experienced a convergence between my love for the Lord's Prayer and my love for music. The result is what I call the "4/4 pattern" of prayer.

In music, the 4/4 pattern is the most basic beat. In adapting the elements of that pattern to the Lord's Prayer, it looks like this:

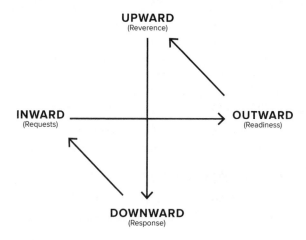

UPWARD
(Reverence)

INWARD
(Requests)

OUTWARD
(Readiness)

DOWNWARD
(Response)

Every time I look at a Biblical text as a springboard to prayer, I think in terms of this pattern. As you think about this pattern, keep in mind that our prayers begin in the Scriptures. So, I always start with an open Bible. Very often, I use a Psalm—but really almost any text of God's Word can initiate our praying, using this pattern. We also know that our teacher is the Holy Spirit. We come to the text with a ready mind but also with our whole being entirely surrendered to the instruction of the Holy Spirit as we pray.

The Starting Place: Reverence

Imagine a conductor before an orchestra. The conductor raises a hand and fixes it high to capture the attention of the musicians. Every member is at full attention. In the prayer pattern Jesus gave His disciples, He instructs us to begin with reverence, an upward focus of worship ("Our Father in Heaven, hallowed be Your name"). In keeping with Jesus' instructions, prayer begins with the character of God as we take time to focus our entire being on the wonders of who God is.

As our Father, He is caring and intimate. As the One who is in Heaven, He is transcendent, holy, and separate. Striking this perfect balance, Jesus teaches us to draw near with assurance and awe, in heartfelt intimacy, holy imagination, and *Abba* adoration. Spending quality time with an opened Bible, delighting in the names and character of God, is the most important engagement in our lives and the vital starting point of prayer.

The Downward Stroke: Response

Next, the musical conductor gives the downbeat, and the composition begins. In this prayer pattern, our "music" of worship and praise has already commenced. Now we respond to God's character. Jesus taught the essence of this when He said, "Your kingdom come. Your will be done on earth as it is in Heaven." This response to God's character in prayer involves yielding to the control of the

Holy Spirit and recommitting ourselves to God's kingdom purposes. Introspection and surrender mark this time of yielding to the Spirit's promptings. It is a season of pledged obedience to the will and Word of God, desiring the accomplishment of His purposes in our lives.

The Inward Stroke: Requests

From the downbeat, the conductor now moves the baton, slanting upward and left, setting the tempo for the music. In prayer, we are now ready to express trust in God for the needs of our lives by way of our *requests*. I often say that we do not really know what to ask for until we have worshiped well and surrendered completely. From this position of spiritual alignment, we come to the Father with our requests. "Give us this day our daily bread. And forgive us our debts, as we forgive our debtors" (Matthew 6) invites us to pray about the *resource* and *relationship* issues of life.

The Outward Stroke: Readiness

As the music continues, the conductor moves the beat to the right, keeping tempo. As our prayer continues, the outward stroke reminds us of the spiritual contest before us and, more importantly, reassures us of the spiritual resources within us. We know the time comes when we must get off our knees and reenter the warfare zone. We must be battle-ready.

When we pray, "Do not lead us into temptation, but deliver us from the evil one," we recognize our own inability to overcome the temptations and snares of daily life. We entrust our welfare for the warfare to the One who is our victor. We are praying to be battle-ready through our trust in Christ.

The Upward Stroke: Reverence

With an upward motion, the conductor returns the beat to the starting point. The traditional version we recite (from the King

James Version of Matthew 6:13), concludes on a high note of praise: "For thine is the kingdom, and the power, and the glory, for ever. Amen." We conclude our prayer with a doxology, an expression giving glory to God. We close the door on prayer the same way we opened it—with praise.

Join us in prayer for Day 16
at www.strategicrenewal.com/21days

This Is How We Do It – Part 1

In the course of this prayer journey, I have become captivated with the sufficiency of God *in* prayer and *for* prayer. Often, as people arrive for these multi-day prayer experiences (usually held at a camp or conference center), they wonder how in the world a group of people is going to pray for hours and days on end. The Lord is always faithful. As I say, "God is always glad to oblige when you give Him your undivided attention."

Of course, a request-based approach would typically run out of steam after twenty minutes, maybe an hour at best. But in the free-flowing dynamic of opening our Bibles, trusting the Spirit's leadership, and allowing all who feel prompted by the Spirit to participate, a full kaleidoscope of prayer options emerges. In fact, for me, this is one of the most beautiful demonstrations of the sufficiency of the Word of God, the Spirit of God, and the people of God in active and practical ministry.

Bible Boogie Board–Holy Spirit Wave

As I travel and speak, it is this confidence that guides me as I engage in an experience I affectionately describe as "grabbing my Bible boogie board and catching the Holy Spirit wave." I lead the group through a process of spontaneously picking a psalm. After reading the psalm together, I lead the people "on the fly" through the steps of the 4/4 pattern, demonstrating how it kindles worship, springing from truths about God. Following a time of spontaneous worship, we then pray from the text with the focus on the other elements of this prayer pattern. The process is always a spiritual adrenaline rush but also so fresh and life-giving.

Practically, I call these the who, how, what, and where questions of practicing this pattern.

- Who is God? (reverence)
- How should I respond? (response)
- What do I pray about? (requests)
- Where do I go from here? (readiness)

Reverence (the Starting Place): Who Is God?

Begin with a psalm or some other portion of Scripture. Because this is a worship-based approach, the first question as you read any passage of Scripture is: "Who is God?" Asked another way, "What does this passage reveal about God and His character?" Invite the Holy Spirit to give you understanding of what the text tells you about the Father, Son, and Holy Spirit.

Begin your prayer time seeking His face in worship, using your own words. You may utilize simple "finish the sentence" prayers like, "I praise You because You are..." Or you may focus on a particular attribute of God, like His power: "God, I have seen Your power..."— then describe the ways He has made His power known to you. Or you might focus on His grace with a prayer that says, "Thank You for showing me Your grace when..." Honor Him for the many indicators of His grace in your life.

Response (the Downward Stroke): How Should I Respond?

Remember, revelation demands response. So, how do you want God's kingdom to come and His will to be done in your life in response to His character? Using cues from the Scripture, you can pray, "Father, be Lord of my..." or "Lord, rule over..." You can submit specific dimensions of your life to His authority—like your mind, emotions, doubts, fears, plans, career, family, ministry, etc. Confess areas of your life that require fresh surrender to His will—like your thought life, friendships, marriage, finances, or children.

Punctuate this time with songs of surrender and humility. If you journal, reflect on what the Lord is putting into your heart during this time. Write specifically about your expressions of submission and yieldedness.

Requests (the Inward Stroke): What Should I Pray About?

If you have a prayer list, you can utilize it here. However, let the passages of Scripture guide you in the articulation of your requests. Many times, a passage will give you practical clues about how you can trust the Lord for the resources and relationships of your life. Maybe the Scripture you are using addresses the issue of fear. You begin to pray, "Lord, I will trust You for my fears about..." Or, you may pray for others, "I pray for __ (name) as they cope with fear in the midst of __ (situation)."

Perhaps the text speaks of various struggles, needs, decisions, challenges, or longings. Turn these into specific prayers of trust as you commit various resource concerns and arenas of relationships to the Lord. It is amazing to see how the Spirit will expose needs and direct your prayers according to the will of God.

Readiness (the Outward Stroke): Where Do I Go from Here?

Toward the end of the prayer time, thoughts tend to move toward the hours, days, or weeks that are before you. The "where?" question simply prompts you to think about the mission of your life and the warfare you can anticipate.

Many texts will speak of some challenge or spiritual enemy to overcome. These cues will guide you in identifying and anticipating practical spiritual battles. Just as Jesus used the memorized Word to defeat Satan, look for a promise or truth that you can pray over the temptations, toils, and snares that await you beyond the door of your prayer room.

Perhaps the text speaks of God's power over His enemies. You might pray, "Lord, I will rely on Your power as I face the enemy, or challenge, of __." Or perhaps there is a promise in the text. You might pray, "Be my victory as I encounter __." Then quote that promise, repeatedly, as you list the battles you might face. It is a great way to integrate Scripture memory into your prayer time as you become battle-ready.

Reverence (the Upward Stroke): Who Is God?

End where you began, with your eyes on Him. You have expressed your reverence in Scripture-fed, Spirit-led worship. You have responded in submission to His kingdom purposes and will. You have trusted Him with requests for the resource and relationship concerns of life. You cultivated readiness in your heart and mind for the battles ahead. Now, with your eyes on Him, declare, "For Yours is the kingdom and the power and the glory forever. Amen" (Matthew 6). This is a great moment to conclude with a song focused on His lordship, power, and glory.

Join us in prayer for Day 17
at www.strategicrenewal.com/21days

This Is How We Do It – Part 2

Now that you have a better idea of how to implement the 4x4, worship-based prayer pattern, let's look at a specific example so you can put this into practice in your own prayer time.

Incidentally, you do not have to pray from an entire chapter of the Bible. Select a portion that is substantive, yet short enough to work for you. I chose First Peter chapter 5 randomly as it is one of the shorter chapters of the New Testament. Please take a few moments to read through this passage right now; then we will look at how you can use this passage with the 4x4, worship-based prayer pattern.

Reverence: Who Is God?

From this text you see that God is:

The suffering Savior—v. 1; God of glory, He lives in glory, He will reveal His glory; He will take us to glory—v. 1; He works in us to give us a willing heart—vv. 2, 3; Chief Shepherd—v. 4; Rewarder—v. 4; Resists the proud—v. 5; Gives grace to the humble—v. 5; Mighty—v. 6; Exalts the humble—v. 6; Cares for us—v. 7; Gives us faith and power to resist the devil—v. 9; God of all grace—v. 10; Eternal—v. 10; Glorious—v. 10; Calls us—v. 10; Redeems our experiences of suffering—v. 10; Perfects, establishes, strengthens, settles—v. 10; Glorious—v. 11; Dominion and rule—v. 11; Gives us grace to stand—v. 12; God of peace—v. 14.

As you can see, there are many ways from this passage to say, "Father in Heaven, hallowed be Your name." A few examples:

- I glorify You (vv. 1, 10, 11) because You are...

- I praise You that you have shown Your grace (v. 5) when. . .

- I worship You because Your hand is mighty (v. 6) over...

Response: How Should I Respond?

Here are some possible prayers of surrender to His purposes and will:

- I surrender my attitudes of "compulsion" and duty (v. 2), asking You to make me willing to...

- I surrender my attitude of greed ("dishonest gain") (v. 2) in _____ (situation).

- Rule over my lack of submission and humility (vv. 5, 6) in _____ (situation).

- Humble my pride of _____ under Your mighty hand (v. 6).

- Even though it is hard, I embrace my suffering (v. 10) in _____ (situation).

Requests: What Should I Pray About?

Again, the Spirit will give you specific insight in the moment as to what you should pray about, but here are a few ideas:

Resources

- I cast my cares (v. 7) about _____ upon You, thanking You that You care for me.

- I pray for _____ as he/she encounters trials (sufferings—v. 10), asking that You would perfect, establish, strengthen, and settle him/her.

Relationships

- Help me to be an example (v. 3) to _____
(names) as I serve them willingly.

- Help _____ (name) to submit to You in his/her
relationship with _____ (name).

- Give _____ (name) humility and grace (v. 5) as
he/she deals with _____ (relationship).

Readiness: Where Do I Go from Here?

Themes about the spiritual battle are obvious in this text. A few prayer ideas include:

- Give me Your grace to be sober/self-controlled and vigilant/
alert as I face the enemy today in _____
(specific trials or temptations).

- Today, I will resist the devil's attacks and stand firm in my
faith, through Your promise of _____
(claim Scripture promises from this text or anywhere in the
Bible; meditate on these promises in light of the battles of
the day).

Reverence: Who Is God?

- Repeat the doxology (v. 11) several times with conviction!
- Praise Him for His peace (v. 14).
- Sing—"It Is Well With My Soul."

Seed Thoughts vs. Spirit Thoughts

The previous examples are just seed thoughts. The Spirit is the teacher, in the moment, in every moment of prayer. The Spirit takes the Word, making our worship soar and causing His Word to flourish in our prayers.

The goal is not to train you in a new technique but to motivate you to a life of prayer, according to the teachings of Christ. My hope is that in the simplicity of this pattern you also sense the sufficiency of the Word and Spirit in your praying and in your living. The goal is that this kind of prayer is woven into the fabric of your life and that your life is woven into the fabric of your praying.

If you would like to practice the 4x4 prayer pattern with a little guidance, our website has prayer guides and prompts for dozens of the Psalms. Visit www.strategicrenewal.com and click on the "prayer guides" tab.

You can also download our Strategic Renewal app (via iTunes or Goggle) to find additional prayer guides and experience guided prayer from the Scriptures.

Join us in prayer for Day 18
at www.strategicrenewal.com/21days

Coming Out of the Prayer Closet

Over two hundred people stood shoulder-to-shoulder, arm-in-arm, hand-in-hand around a beautifully decorated Communion table. Tears flowed from radiant faces. Some looked Heavenward while others worshiped with eyes closed. In angelic harmony, our voices resounded in the final verse of "All Hail the Power of Jesus' Name."

Every time I enjoy these experiences of extraordinary corporate prayer, I am reminded that transformation is not something that occurs only in privacy. It is also fueled by praying in community with others. I could not wrap up this book without a strong challenge to find transformational prayer in community to complement your personal prayer journey.

Individual + Community = Transformation

We know that God wants our prayers to be transformational. If you were to ask, "Which is more important, private prayer or corporate prayer?" My answer would always be "yes"! It's like asking which leg is more crucial to walking—the right or the left?

In the Early Church, they understood the value of community—meeting together daily in prayer and the other vital disciplines for spiritual growth (Acts 2:42). The Church was birthed in a ten-day prayer meeting (Acts 1:14; 2:1). They coped with crisis and persecution together, on their knees (Acts 4:24–31).

What a contrast to our individualized culture. Most of us were taught that prayer is something we do almost exclusively on our own in a closet somewhere. In reality, early Christians learned to pray largely by praying together.

Personally, I cannot imagine living a vibrant and balanced Christian life without a regular dose of both. Those who neglect the consistent habit of praying in extended fashion with a community of believers are robbing themselves of great blessing and balance. In a sense, they are trying to hop on one leg and finding the prayer journey difficult, at best.

Group Instruction

We've looked at the Lord's Prayer as a model for the *content* of our praying. We should also embrace it as a model for the *context* of our prayers. Jesus said to His followers in Matthew 6:5, "And when you pray...." He assumed they would gather in prayer as a regular part of their spiritual development. The pronoun here is plural, as Jesus is talking to them as a group about their engagement in prayer as a group. In our language, it would be "when you guys pray" or "when y'all pray" (in Southern dialect). In other words, Jesus says, "When you all pray together as My followers, do it this way in your gatherings, not like those praise-hungry Pharisees or misguided Gentiles."

To support this idea, the pronouns are all plural in the pattern of prayer He gave. He did not give the instruction to pray, "*My* Father in Heaven... give *Me* this day *My* daily bread, and forgive *Me My* debts... Do not lead *Me* into temptation, but deliver *Me* from the evil one..." Instead, this was a teaching passage on the mindset, motives, venue, and pattern of corporate praying in the lives of Jesus' followers.

Many believers struggle in learning how to pray. Hundreds of volumes have been written over the centuries on the theology and practice of prayer. Yet the most fundamental principle has often been neglected. Young Christians must learn to pray in community with mature believers. Prayer is vital for transformation, and corporate prayer is indispensable as a part of the process.

If I Were the Devil

I recently wrote a devotion titled "If I Were the Devil." I noted that while the devil is NOT all-knowing, he is brilliant, supernatural, and shrewd from thousands of years of experience. He certainly knows some things. He knows the Bible (James 2:19–20), so he knows the divine game plan for his defeat—and the vital role of prayer.

He knows Church history. He is fully aware that his greatest defeats have come during seasons of spiritual awakening and revival and that every one of these seasons of exponential spiritual transformation has been rooted in movements of united, Biblical prayer.

He also knows human nature. He observes our tendency to live independently of God's supernatural provision for our lives. He likes things this way.

Therefore, if I were the devil, I would use my best deceptive tools to keep Christians from praying in transforming ways—and especially to keep them from praying together. I would keep them busy and isolated from one another. I would do everything possible to keep them distracted and disinterested in Biblical, balanced, revival-style prayer gatherings.

To accomplish this, I would do the following:

- Fuel the spirit of rugged individualism.

- Dig ruts of boring prayer.

- Delight in theological orthodoxy without spiritual passion.

- Encourage idle preaching on prayer.

- Promote "success" in the ministry (instead of true broken-
ness and repentance).

Yes, if I were the devil, this strategy would be one of my most important. I would amass all of my most subtle and deceptive troops and tools to prevent transforming prayer and spiritual awakening at all costs. As long as Christians were sincere but isolated, active but powerless, entertained but shallow, I would win.

Jesus' Plan: United in Transformation

In spite of the devil's malevolent intentions, the Lord Jesus has a triumphant, supernatural plan, and we must embrace it with re-solve. In Mark 11:17, Jesus made His intentions clear: "Then He taught, saying to them, 'Is it not written, "My house shall be called a house of prayer for all nations"? But you have made it a "den of thieves.""" Jesus knew the kind of power He was able to unleash in humble, dependent people who would allow Him to bear the fruit of His life and power through prayer. Again, that is why He started the Church with His people on their knees. He sustained and blessed the Church the same way. Still today, He wants His Church to be characterized by an environment of life-giving prayer.

When we pray together in a worship-based fashion, not only is God glorified in our very act of collective adoration but also in our ongoing recognition of His transforming power, both in and through us as He advances His Gospel and glory in this world.

Join us in prayer for Day 19
at www.strategicrenewal.com/21days

The Privileges, Possibilities, and Provision Related to Prayer

I have heard it said that nothing is dynamic until it is specific. To say that the power and potential of prayer is dynamic is an understatement tantamount to saying the sun is bright and hot. Yet specificity fuels deeper appreciation. Before we end this 21-day journey, let's remind our hearts again of the many positive realities of Biblical prayer.

Counting the blessings and benefits of prayer can ignite fresh vision and passion for what Christ can do in us, for us, and through us when we seriously embrace the privilege. Let's take a moment to consider the privileges, explore the possibilities, and imagine the provision available to us because of God's gift of prayer to our hearts.

Prayer Has Its Privileges

Consider the privileges available to us in prayer:

- In prayer, we experience the most intimate and powerful spiritual exercise known to humanity (Psalm 131; Romans 8:14; Galatians 4:6).

- In prayer, we talk freely about our secret struggles, frustrated feelings, and our murky motives with words that are raw and unfiltered—yet understood by an all-knowing, all-powerful God (Psalm 62:8; Hebrews 4:16).

- In prayer, we find protection when we are vulnerable and experience security when we are unsure (Psalm 34:4; 56:3; 2 Corinthians 1:8–11).

- In prayer, we accept our weaknesses, surrender our rights, and ask for help from the only One who can create permanent change (2 Chronicles 20:12; Psalm 40:17; Luke 22:42; 2 Corinthians 12:8–10).

- In prayer, we abide through intimate connection to the life-giving power of the risen Christ (John 15:4–5; Ephesians 3:16–19; Colossians 1:9–10).

- In prayer, we trade in our anxieties for the peace that passes all understanding (Psalm 29:11; Isaiah 26:3; Philippians 4:6–7).

- In prayer, we receive wisdom for the perplexities and doubts we face (2 Chronicles 1:10; Proverbs 2:3–6; James 1:5).

- In prayer, we cast our burdens on the One who has the power to work all things out for our good and His glory (Psalm 55:22; Romans 8:26–28; 1 Peter 5:7).

- In prayer, desperate and lost people receive mercy and grace that saves and transforms (Luke 18:13; Romans 10:13).

- In prayer, faith grows and God's people arise to call on Him boldly for miraculous exploits from His hand (Jeremiah 33:3; Mark 9:23–24; 11:23–24; Acts 12:5–8).

- In prayer, we receive grace to become like Christ, even when the problems persist and the burdens remain (2 Corinthians 3:18; 12:9–10).

- In prayer, we find the power and perseverance to defeat Satan and overcome his schemes (Luke 22:32; Ephesians 6:18; James 4:7).

- In prayer, we discover the beauty and power of intimacy and satisfaction in God (Psalm 27:4, 8; 73:25–26).

Explore the Possibilities

Consider the possibilities available through prayer:

- In prayer, believers discover a level of trust and unity of heart that is truly supernatural, given our many differences in perspective and personality (Acts 1:14; 13:1–2).

- In prayer, families receive grace, health, and persevering love to sacrifice and stay together (Psalm 127; Acts 16:31–34).

- In prayer, God prompts, prepares, and propels Christians to become actively engaged in His evangelistic mission in this world (Matthew 9:38; Acts 4:31; 13:1–3).

- In prayer, leaders receive supernatural insight into the truth of God's Word and wisdom for shepherding His people (Acts 6:2–4; Acts 13:1–2).

- In prayer, major revivals have been birthed, leading to dramatic and lasting transformation of lives, churches, communities, and nations (Acts 6:7).

- In prayer, we receive boldness, wisdom, and opportunities to share the truth of the Gospel (Ephesians 6:18–20; Colossians 4:3–4).

- In prayer, God works powerfully to bring glory to Himself, not through human efforts but through humble dependence (2 Chronicles 20:18–23; John 17; 2 Corinthians 1:10–11).

Provision in Abundance

Consider the provision God has made for us to pray:

- For prayer, Christ went to the cross, offering His life and blood, demonstrating the price that was paid for the privilege of prayer (Ephesians 2:18; Hebrews 10:12–14).

- For prayer, the Temple veil was miraculously torn in two to demonstrate the availability of the Presence and power of God through the finished work of Christ (Matthew 27:50–51; Hebrews 6:19–20; 10:19–22).

• For prayer, sinful hearts are cleansed and become permanent temples of His Spirit, who teaches and guides us to deeper intimacy and greater power (Romans 8:15–17; 26–27; 1 Corinthians 2:9–12).

• For prayer, Jesus now lives, making perpetual intercession for us before the Father, as our sympathetic high priest, that our prayers might be heard and answered (Romans 8:34; Hebrews 7:25; 1 John 2:1–2).

• For prayer, the very Holy of Holies is now open 24/7 with a welcome sign that says to every true believer, "Enter boldly!" (Hebrews 4:14–16; 10:19–22).

Join us in prayer for Day 20
at www.strategicrenewal.com/21days

Your Role in Organic Revival

Imagine waking up one morning to discover these front-page headlines in papers across the nation:

- *Detroit News*: Three Islamic Mullahs and Dozens of Other Muslim Leaders Join Christian Churches

- *Washington Post*: Five Jewish Priests Leave Synagogue to Follow Jesus After Dramatic Conversion

- *Seattle Times*: Surveys Show Bible Sales Up 200% in Recent Weeks

- *San Francisco Chronicle*: Bill Maher Apologizes to Christians After Becoming Born Again

- *Miami Herald*: Adult Book Stores Closing Across Region After Dramatic Downturn in Sales

- *Denver Post*: Churches in Area Boom with Record Attendance; Religious Leaders Cannot Explain Why

Could these things really happen? Is the transforming power of Jesus Christ still able to accomplish such exploits? Does it stir your heart to dream of being a part of this kind of movement of God's Spirit?

What Sparks Revival?

If you examine Acts 6 to see what sparked this amazing movement of the Spirit, you will not find three quick steps to church growth. The solution rested in two important decisions. First, the leaders resolved not to jump in and design a new program. Instead, they said, "We will give ourselves continually to prayer and to the ministry of the word" (Act 6:4). Second, they had an authentic confidence in the sufficiency of the Spirit in the people to resolve the problem through the selection of a godly team of coordinators. God blessed their faith and unleashed a whole new wave of spiritual power that advanced the Gospel in exponential fashion.

The Apostles knew if this environment was to grow, they had to lead it by their own example. They dedicated great amounts of their time to praying together and leading the Church in seeking the Lord. Sadly, today, we have a different scenario in most churches. Leaders have become program designers, savvy administrators, and problem solvers. The people generally sit, soak, and sour as they watch the professionals run the show. The power we see in Acts 6:1–7 captures a different picture.

We need an Acts 6 revival. Revival is not a week of evangelistic meetings or a televised healing crusade. It is a period of unusual blessing when God brings a supernatural re-enlivening to His people. History shows that whenever God wanted to bring a great work of revival, He always began by sending His people to their knees. We see this principle in 2 Chronicles 7:14 ("If My people... will humble themselves, and pray and seek My face..."), and we see it demonstrated in a fresh wave of power here in Acts 6:1–7.

Can We Organize an Awakening?

These days, it seems everyone is trying to drum up excitement for another revival event or program. There is no shortage of ideas afloat about how we all need to converge at some big gathering to get a transforming touch among the masses that have traveled far and wide to find a new angle on prayer and renewal. Some of these gatherings are designed to call down God's fire; others focus on the need to wait quietly on some new revelation. I am sure the organizers are sincere and certainly dedicated. Each has some Biblical guidelines that motivate all the activity. Certainly, God can use these events for His glory.

Yet all are expensive and complicated to organize. Honestly, I find myself wondering if this is really the Lord's best plan for reviving His Church. In the rush of getting God to show up at another revival event, I wonder if we might not need to slow down, tone down, and get down to the humble, quiet, grassroots spiritual transformation that revivals are made of in intimacy and obscurity.

Dreaming Organic

I am dreaming of something more organic. I hope you will too. *Organic* refers to something "arising as a natural outgrowth." The vision for organic revival that moves my heart today looks like this: "Pastor-led, local church-oriented movements of Christ-exalting, worship-based prayer—leading to a full-scale revival, supernatural evangelism, and cultural transformation." My friends call it my hyper-hyphenated vision. Put more simply, it is to see the next Great Awakening in our generation.

Essentially, this is what drives my desire to equip individuals and pastors to experience transforming prayer in the context of life. It is the longing to see churches become houses of prayer, distinguished by spiritual passion and endurance. The goal is clearly not the elevation of any church, ministry, or personality but that Christ would receive glory as congregations around the nation awaken to His Presence and purposes. It is worship-based prayer that cultivates a deep repentance in His Presence, a growing desperation for His power, and an unquenchable passion for His renown.

I believe as pastors embrace an extraordinary commitment to prayer and His Word (Acts 6:4), and believers engage in experiences of transforming prayer, a full-scale revival could occur in the environment of praying churches. The water-level of awakening would rise. Congregations in the North, South, East, and West—large and small, and of various denominational stripes—would experience His glory. Out of this movement, profound evangelism would occur, as it historically occurred in previous revivals. Ultimately, our culture would be transformed by the Gospel as manifested through a glorious Church. Then the tide would turn.[1]

Change Starts Now

You can be a vital part of this compelling and essential vision. Ultimately, this kind of revival starts with my heart, my home, my church, and my community. If you pray that for me—and I pray that for you—and we act in faith to seek His face, something organic and glorious might just occur. It is worth dreaming about, worth seeking after, and worth living for.

My friend Byron Paulus says, "The biggest billboard for revival is a changed life." That is the beautiful outcome of transforming prayer. Thanks for joining me in the journey. May God be magnified!

Join us in prayer for Day 21
at www.strategicrenewal.com/21days

Epilogue

Now What?

I hope you have enjoyed this 21-Day journey. I trust you have been blessed by praying along with Alice, Jim, and me. You might be wondering about next steps. Let me offer some important recommendations.

- If you have taken this journey individually, now invite others to join you in a second time through. Invite a spouse, a prayer partner, your family, your small group, or your entire church to experience these truths together and truly "get on the same prayer page" together.

- If you want to go deeper, purchase the full book, *Transforming Prayer: How Everything Changes When You Seek God's Face* and absorb the additional, rich content of the original teaching that has helped scores of thousands of other believers.

- Better yet, use the book along with the *Transforming Prayer* small group video series available at the www.strategicrenewal.com online bookstore.

- Sign up for our *Monday Motivator* at www.strategicrenewal.com. You can get fresh content every Monday to enrich your walk with the Lord and inspire your prayer life.

- If you are a pastor, you really *MUST* join *The 6:4 Fellowship* to discover rich resources and deeper community with other pastors in "Prayer-and-word-powered-ministry." Sign up for free at www.64fellowship.com.

Notes

DAY 1: Beyond a "Grocery List" of Needs

1. J. Oswald Sanders, Prayer Power Unlimited (Chicago: Moody Press, 1977), 11.

DAY 3: What Is Blocking the Breakthrough?

1. "Study shows only 16 percent of Protestant ministers are very satisfied with their personal prayer lives," Grey Matter Research, www.greymatterresearch.com/index_files/Prayer.htm.

DAY 7: The Case of the Missing Prayer List

1. Perhaps the most extensive "prayer list" is found in 1 Timothy 2:1–5, where Paul writes, "Therefore I exhort first of all that supplications, prayers, intercessions, and giving of thanks be made for all men, for kings and all who are in authority, that we may lead a quiet and peaceable life in all godliness and reverence. For this is good and acceptable in the sight of God our Savior, who desires all men to be saved and to come to the knowledge of the truth." The emphasis here is a variety of prayer expressions focused on societal leadership and a believer's responsibility to live in ways that adorn the Gospel, with an ultimate goal of evangelism.

DAY 8: All Prayer Requests Are Not Created Equal

1. John Franklin, And the Place Was Shaken—How to Lead a Powerful Prayer Meeting (Nashville: Broadman and Holman, 2005), 33–34.

DAY 11: How Abiding Guides Our Asking

1. Calvin Miller, The Path to Celtic Prayer (Downers Grove, IL: InterVarsity Press, 2007), 57.

2. Charles Spurgeon, as cited in A 12-Month Guide to Better Prayer (Uhrichsville, OH: Barbour Publishing, 2009), 38.

3. Taken from a recent e-mail but based on Bud McCord's excellent book The Satisfying Life, www.thesatisfyinglife.com.

4. John Piper sermon, "How to Pray for a Desolate Church," January 5, 1992, www.desiringgod.org.

DAY 12: How His Spirit Ignites Our Supplication

1. Kenneth S. Wuest, Ephesians and Colossians in the Greek New Testament (Grand Rapids: Eerdmans, 1953), 145.

2. John Piper sermon, "Learning to Pray in the Spirit and the Word"—Part 2, January 7, 2001, www.desiringgod.org.

DAY 13: How His Name Corrects Our Nonsense

1. Helen H. Lemmel, "Turn Your Eyes Upon Jesus," 1922. Public domain.

2. W. Bingham Hunter, The God Who Hears (Downers Grove, IL: InterVarsity Press, 1986), 198.

3. Ibid., 198.

4. I now begin my prayers in this fashion, "Father, in Jesus Name, and by Your indwelling Spirit." This frontloads all that I am about to say with a deeper awareness of Jesus' character and will with the assurance of the Spirit's role in the prayer I am about to pray.

DAY 16: Transforming Prayer for Dummies

1. John MacArthur, Jesus' Pattern of Prayer (Chicago: Moody Press, 1981), 10.

DAY 21: Your Role in Organic Revival

1. This is the vision of The 6:4 Fellowship. For more information, go to www.64fellowship.com.

Acknowledgements

Special thanks to:

My wife, Rosemary, for always supporting me and the work to which God has called me.

Tony Brown for spearheading this project from the start.

Jennell Houts for her excellent editing work.

Jim Maxim and Alice Moss for the contribution of their passionate prayers.

Jay Phelps for the excellent cover art.

Carley Phelps and the Strategic Renewal staff for moving the project forward.

The team at Bethany Press in the final work of layout, design, and printing.

About the Contributors

Daniel Henderson served as a Senior Pastor for over two decades, bringing prayer-based revitalization to numerous churches. Now, as the President of Strategic Renewal, Daniel is dedicating his full-time efforts to help congregations across the country and world experience renewal. Daniel is sought after for his communication gifts and expertise in leading corporate prayer. He has authored numerous books on Biblical leadership and prayer, including, *Old Paths, New Power* and *Transforming Prayer: How Everything Changes When You Seek God's Face.*

Jim Maxim is the Chairman and founder of MaximTrak Technologies, an International Software Firm serving the automotive and power sports industries as well as President and founder of Maxim

Automotive, which specializes in forming and managing re-insurance companies for automotive dealers. Jim and his wife Cathy have been involved in inner city ministry for over 30 years as regular hosts of city-wide prayer gatherings and founders of Acts 4:13 (a ministry dedicated to mobilizing the church to prayer for pastors). He is also an author and public speaker.

Alice Moss is a Bible teacher, retreat speaker, workshop leader, and worship-based prayer facilitator. She has a unique ability to reach women with her genuine, enthusiastic love for Jesus. She offers wise Biblical counsel to women based on a mature and clear understanding of God's Word. She recently authored a biographical book, *I Crossed Over*, which recounts her own 40-year journey in prayer for her husband's salvation.

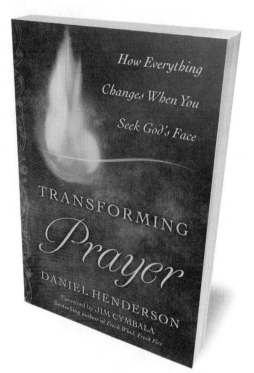

When you experience the profound difference of worship-based prayer, your faith and life will never be the same.

It's no wonder so many people are discouraged with prayer. Instead of a genuine encounter with God, prayer is little more than a grocery list of requests. Maybe you, too, seek God's hand rather than His face. How do you truly connect with God through prayer? In his full book, Transforming Prayer, Daniel Henderson will show you how to overcome common barriers to praying effectively, awaken your prayer life with simple, biblical patterns of prayer, and enjoy Spirit-led prayer sparked by Scripture passages. Take your prayer life from ordinary to extraordinary!

Also available as an eBook and audiobook.

BETHANY HOUSE

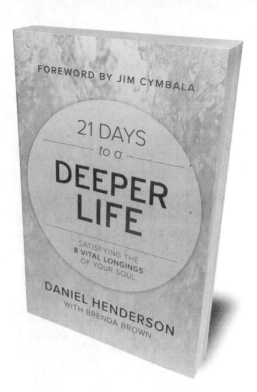

Escape the fog of daily distractions and unfulfilled goals.

Daniel Henderson helps you live with greater focus and intentionality, in this daily, devotional format. Your step-by-step guide to daily spiritual renewal.

The Deeper Life material helps you find personal and Biblical answers to the 8 vital questions everyone asks including:

• Who is God? (Theology)
• Who am I? (Identity)
• Why am I here? (Purpose)

Includes 21 daily readings along with application questions and an audio prayer to follow along with each day.

Purchase at: store.strategicrenewal.com

STRATEGIC RENEWAL

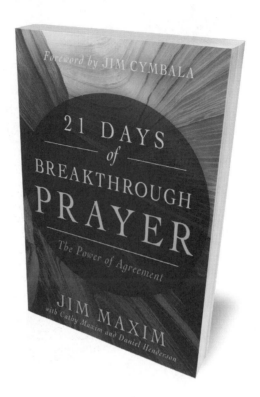

Are there things in your personal life, your loved ones' lives, or your church life that desperately need to change for the better?

Have you been yearning for real spiritual breakthrough in the challenging situations you face? Have you ever considered that God is just waiting for His people to cry out to Him in prayer together?

More than just a book printed on paper, this 21-day movement is interactive. At the end of each devotional reading, you can join Jim, Cathy, and Daniel for a powerful time of agreeing prayer online. See how different things can be as believers go to God together to experience a time of intimacy and intercession that will forever change the way we pray, think, and act regarding the gift of prayer.

WHITAKER HOUSE